ALSO BY PAT BAIRD

The Pyramid Cookbook

QUICK
AND
HEARTY

Meatless Microwave Meals
Everyone Will Enjoy

Pat Baird

An Owl Book
Henry Holt and Company
New York

Henry Holt and Company, Inc.
Publishers since 1866
115 West 18th Street
New York, New York 10011

Henry Holt® is a registered
trademark of Henry Holt and Company, Inc.

Library of Congress Cataloging-in-Publication Data
Baird, Pat.
[Quick harvest]
Quick and hearty : meatless microwave meals everyone will enjoy /
Pat Baird. — 1st Owl Book ed.
p.   cm.
"Owl book."
Originally published: Quick Harvest. New York : Prentice Hall
Press, 1991.
Includes index.
1. Vegetarian cookery.   2. Microwave cookery.   I. Title.
TX837.B2186   1995   94-41784
641.5'636—dc20   CIP

ISBN 0-8050-3743-8

Henry Holt books are available for special promotions
and premiums. For details contact: Director, Special Markets.

First published in hardcover in 1991 by Prentice Hall Press.

First Owl Book Edition—1995

Designed by Barbara Cohen Aronica

Printed in the United States of America
All first editions are printed on acid-free paper.∞

10 9 8 7 6 5 4 3 2 1

The recipe for Yogurt is adapted from *101 Microwaving Secrets* by Barbara Methven. Copyright
© 1982 by Cy DeCosse Incorporated. Reprinted by permission of Cy DeCosse, Inc.

Stephen's Bread Pudding adapted from the recipe in *Master Recipes* by Stephen Schmidt.
Copyright © 1981 by Stephen Schmidt. Reprinted by permission of Fawcett Books, published by
Ballantine Books, a division of Random House, Inc.

Mushrooms and Leeks and Lombardy Custard are adapted from recipes in *To the King's Taste:
Richard II's Book of Feasts & Recipes Adapted for Modern Cooking*. Copyright © 1975 by Lorna J.
Sass. Reprinted by permission of The Metropolitan Museum of Art.

ACKNOWLEDGMENTS

I've learned that writing a book is never a solitary event, and so to the many people who helped make this book possible, I'd like to express my personal appreciation.

Marilyn Abraham, at our first meeting, said she suspected that I have many books in me; I knew that some day we would work together. Now at Prentice Hall Press we did.

Madeline Morel, my agent, wanted me to do a vegetarian book from the start, believed in it, and then helped me to develop a winning proposal.

Toula Polygalaktos, my editor, is without a doubt the best editor that any author could ever hope to have. I am delighted that we were able to work together and happier that I have found a new friend.

To my three "private editors" who were always there for me, above and beyond the call of duty, my deepest appreciation. Kathy Leonard lent her professional skills as an editor to look at the manuscript and spent hours with me on the phone giving her comments and support. Barbara Reiss, my neighbor, always had the time to read, edit, taste, comment, console, and has been one of my strongest supporters. Lorna Sass, my dear friend and colleague, convinced me that I could and should write this book. She has shared much of her time, knowledge, skill, and love to shape this book, and has shaped a good part of my life as well. In the very final hour, once again it was Lorna to the rescue as she named this book.

Thanks also to my friends who graciously contributed in a variety of ways:

Helen Berman, for reasons I can hardly begin to enumerate, but to whom I will be ever grateful for so many things.

Keith Brownfield built my L.A. office with fine care and detail and made it perfect in every way; and also understood that sometimes there was just no stopping (where I was) or what I was doing.

Mike Center developed some great recipes for these pages and was always ready to go to the next step to help me out.

Arthur Charurat skillfully built my microwave table while Marilyn cheered him on.

Carol Gelles generously and enthusiastically asked to index this book, and did a splendid job.

Barbara Hansen, a talented food writer, has become a close friend and never let more that twenty-four hours pass without giving me a response to any of my questions and has always been right there to cheer me on.

Dana Jacobi generously gave her time and knowledge to teach me more about tempeh than I ever dreamed possible.

Lester Noriel, my computer consultant, may be one of the kindest and most understanding people in the world. He has allowed me to badger him whenever "disk distress" set in.

Dave Yanis's spontaneous calculations always reminded me of exactly where I was, and precisely what I needed to do to finish.

On the professional and industry side I was inspired by the assistance of many generous people.

Thelma Pressman and Thelma Snyder, warmly greeted me into the microwave world and their circle of authors.

Linda Funk, of the Wisconsin Milk Marketing Board; Nadia Kamin, of the Rice Council; Cliff Larsen, of the Hershey Foods Corporation; Sky Stanton, of Golin Harris (on behalf of Dow); Susan Masten and Nora Connellan, of Dorf & Stanton (on behalf of Sharp Electronics), devoted their time, patience, and care to my questions, and obtained whatever technical information I needed.

The partners of the Law Offices of Harris & Baird, separately and collectively, allowed their practice to be interrupted with microwave oven deliveries and recipe samplings (even though food is not permitted in the office); and lent computer and secretarial support for the typing of the manuscript. Hattie Harris took time during one of her biggest trials to test and supply the recipe for her famous Cranberry Sauce. Rita Baird, her partner and my sister, planted a wonderful garden of vegetables and herbs so that I would have ready access to fresh produce for the recipes. She turned over her home, her kitchen, and a good part of her life to make this book happen. A new element of our relationship developed as she showered me with love and I felt her pride in me as her sister and as her friend.

Special thanks to Buddy for giving up his truck—albeit reluctantly—for an entire summer, and to Doc for never turning down an invitation for recipe sampling.

Few authors deliver a manuscript without the help of a typist: I was fortunate enough to have two. And here ultimate credit must be given. Susanne Speranza, in New York, has never let me miss a deadline on this or any other project. Beryl

Cooper, in Los Angeles, truly made this manuscript her own. Be it weekends, during or after hours, Beryl was helpful, enthusiastic, and always reminded me that "It will get done," (and it did!). My special gratitude for her personal dedication and hard work, but most of all for giving me the gift of laughter . . . when I least expected it.

And finally, to all the many, many others who have helped me, guided me, and loved me. Thanks for being there.

My sincere thanks and gratitude go also to the following organizations who were so generous with their equipment, products, time, and information: Corning Glass Corporation; Nordic Ware; Rubbermaid, Incorporated; Litton Systems, Inc.; Sharp Electronics; Sunbeam Appliance Company; Toshiba America; International Micro-wave Power Institute; American Spice Trade Association; California Strawberry Board; Eden Foods, Inc.; Frieda's Finest/Produce Specialties, Inc.; Kerr Glass Manufacturing; National Dairy Board; National Potato Board; Ocean Spray Cranberries; Produce Manufacturer's Association; Rice Council of America; and USA Dry Pea and Lentil Industry.

CONTENTS

QUICK
AND
HEARTY

INTRODUCTION

"This was really a great dinner," remarked one of my guests after a meal of recipes that I was testing for this book. "It didn't seem like vegetarian food."

I then asked him what his idea of vegetarian food was. (This is a man who tries to eat in a healthy manner; he also frequents a yoga center where excellent vegetarian meals are served, so this way of eating is hardly new to him.) "Well," he replied, "I think of it as being more sparse and somewhat less satisfying; yet I didn't feel at all that way tonight."

And so it goes. My friend, like many other people, has a somewhat distorted and confused idea of what vegetarian food is. Likewise, few realize how creative vegetarian cooking can be with such delicious results. Being a vegetarian is often surrounded by a cloud of mystery. Some of the ingredients used in food preparation have unfamiliar names and are often only available in health-food or other specialty stores.

So before I go any further, it's important to let you know exactly what this book is all about. Then I think you'll be able to see how vegetarian cooking is different from what you might have expected and how it can appeal to just about everybody who likes to cook and, of course, who likes to eat.

None of the recipes in this book contain meat, chicken, or fish. Many do, however, contain milk, cheese, and other dairy products; many don't. There are several recipes containing tofu, as well as some of the newer grains like quinoa and teff that enhance protein quality. The dessert recipes contain sugar and unbleached white flour as well as molasses and whole wheat flour. Just about all the ingredients are readily available in most supermarkets and require few trips to a health-food store.

Though this book is meant to appeal to vegetarians, I had a broader audience in mind when writing it. Now all those who are caught up in the enthusiasm and pursuit of a healthy lifestyle can have a fast, easy resource from which to prepare their meals.

Nutritional information abounds, and there is just as much misinformation as there is good, solid, sensible data. Whatever their exposure has been most people do accept that there is a strong relationship between the way we eat and the way we feel.

Complex carbohydrates, fresh rather than processed foods, low fat, less meat, and more meatless meals are the guidelines often recommended. But actually putting them into place in our everyday lives, and doing so in a way that is also fast and flavorful, is quite a challenge. For many, it's confusing and overwhelming.

It is for these readers, especially, that I intended this book. I hope they will forget any notion they have had about vegetarian food: That it is bland and overcooked or that it is "rabbit food." What is wonderful about vegetarian food is that it draws from every culture that has ever been present on this earth, and so it is rich with color, flavor, and texture.

Those who are more serious vegetarians may already be enjoying the pleasures of Indian, Italian, and Oriental dishes as part of their daily menus. These, along with Thai, Greek, Mexican, Middle Eastern, and, of course, down-home American dishes will give you a wide variety of interesting meals. Chances are that you enjoy a great many of them already but have just never considered them "vegetarian."

The real magic of the book, though, is the microwave oven. Probably no other style of eating is more suited to microwave food preparation than vegetarian. There is no argument that vegetables and fruits are the crowning glory of the microwave. Because of their high water content they retain color, texture, flavor, and nutritional value in the most outstanding way. Team them up with those complex carbohydrates—whole grains, cereals, rice, pasta, potatoes, beans, peas, lentils— and fresh or dried spices and herbs, and the results are stunning every time. Of course, the speed of the microwave creates these winning combinations in a flash.

The main purpose of the book is to provide meatless recipes for appetizers through desserts, for breakfast, lunch, dinner, and snacks that are fun, interesting, colorful, flavorful, and quick.

As a nutritionist, however, I could not help but include some basic nutrition information to be sure that you started—or continued—your pursuit in a more healthful way. This material and some sensible guidelines for vegetarian eating are included in a separate chapter. All too often I see or hear about people who boast of having given up meat and perhaps all animal products only to turn up anemic, tired, and prone to colds and infection several months later. Clearly, this is the result of poorly chosen eating patterns. Generally it comes from sheer lack of information and proper planning, not from lack of intelligence.

The chapter "Checklist for Healthy Eating" will help get you started, or keep you on a steady course, by providing practical pointers for combining proteins and ensuring an adequate supply of vitamins and minerals for good health.

Because many people may be unfamiliar with microwave cooking or, more than likely, use the microwave only to defrost or to reheat convenience foods and leftovers, several brief chapters on microwave accessories and tips and techniques are also included.

Occasionally I have included a brand name for a product, but only if I thought it might be an unfamiliar one or if others in the same category—like cocoa powder—might give different results. When mentioned, those were the items used to develop and test these recipes.

I hope that you will enjoy this book as much as I have enjoyed writing it. For some it will be an adventure in eating, for many it will be an adventure in cooking. Even the longtime microwave owner may have done little, if any, cooking in the it. Here's your chance.

LAYING THE
GROUNDWORK

My initial experiences with the microwave started out as an adventure. My sister was the first person I knew who actually owned a microwave oven and I wasn't particularly impressed by it at the time. If I think back hard enough, I must admit I was probably a bit intimidated because I couldn't figure out exactly how it worked. After all, it never got hot yet food would scorch and overcook in a wink. It did a dandy job of reheating leftovers and was all right for defrosting foods, so why not just leave it at that. Besides, with a fine range and a good oven, who really needed it?

Then came graduate school. Food science and meal management were among the courses I was required to take in the nutrition master's program. I loved food science and being in the food lab. There was a big old microwave tucked away in the corner of the room which didn't really work—and which the instructors ignored more than talked about!

Several years later when I was teaching food science at the same university, I decided it was time for the students—and me—to learn what these ovens were all about. I called two manufacturers and inquired about a demonstration. They both responded enthusiastically, and soon after we had home economists in the lab with the newest models of their company's ovens.

In less than an hour the class and I had learned the basics in microwave technology, operation, and maintenance and were munching on goodies the home economists had prepared while talking to us. I was mesmerized; the adventure had begun.

Shortly thereafter, a friend of mine got a brand new microwave, similar to one of the models that was brought to the class. I couldn't resist the opportunity to try it out firsthand and actually cook a meal, so I volunteered to prepare dinner for him. "Make it simple; make it work," I said to myself. So dinner that night was poached scallops, buttered broccoli, and salad.

It's amazing how some memories stand out. I can still remember how carefully I mapped out my steps, sequence, and timing according to what I was making. The vegetables needed a high setting with little water and a tight cover but with just enough of an opening to vent the steam which would build up during cooking. On the other hand, the delicate scallops needed gentle cooking and a medium setting would be fine. In both cases I had to watch that the foods were not totally cooked since that would happen during "standing time"—those few minutes when foods continue to cook as the action of the microwaves slows down.

In less than twenty minutes dinner was on the table and we were both astounded. Never had we seen broccoli that was so vibrantly green. It was tender-crisp and for just "plain, buttered broccoli" the flavor was delectable. The scallops were ethereal: juicy, soft, and better than any we had ever had.

I can't describe how delighted I was at the time. Though I had done much more elaborate cooking in a conventional oven and stove and made foods considerably more complicated, this was a major accomplishment to me. Now I knew that it really was possible to cook in a microwave oven. Reheating leftovers from the Mexican restaurant was a thing of the past. In a way I was a student again and a whole new arena had opened up to me.

The point of my story is to let you know that if you take a little time to understand what microwaves are and how they work, you can virtually ensure your success every time. The best and most encouraging part is that the concepts are really quite simple. Once you familiarize yourself with them, you'll be cooking like a pro in no time at all.

After the basics, you will find some hints which can make the whole process even easier. These are included in the chapter "Tips and Techniques" (page 19). Before moving on, let's look at some of the fundamentals and get you set for success.

WHAT ARE MICROWAVES?

Everyone knows that micro means small. Microwaves are tiny, invisible electromagnetic waves that travel at the speed of light. They are a way of transmitting energy just as electricity is electrical energy transmitted through a wire.

Like radio or television waves, microwaves are nonionizing radiant energy. They are not ionizing X rays that cause a chemical change—other than the heat that they produce. This means that they cannot break apart. They do not accumulate or leave residual energy in food, air, or the body. In other words, there is no danger associated with microwaves.

HOW DO MICROWAVES COOK?

Everything in the universe is composed of atoms and molecules. Some of these have electrical charges that can be positive or negative though most have a neutral charge. Water is an important molecule because it is both positive and negative and thus can be very active in a microwave field. It is important to keep in mind that fat and sugar will also attract microwaves. This means that foods containing either fat or sugar will tend to cook faster in the microwave oven.

When microwaves enter the oven through the magnetron tube, they are reflected, passed through, or absorbed by different materials. They are traveling at the speed of light, so all this action causes the molecules in the foods to get very excited and dance around, so to speak. It is the activation of these molecules in the food that causes energy to be dissipated in the form of heat. As the heat builds up, cooking occurs.

Microwaves are very short, only about 3 to 5 inches in length. Usually microwaves penetrate food to a depth of 1 to 1½ inches. Beyond that the food is cooked by conduction, that is, by the heat that has built up on the surface and has been conducted to the food beneath. That's why microwaved foods may be somewhat cooler on their surfaces than an inch or so below them.

The concept of "standing time" is important to keep in mind. Remember that all the atoms and molecules in the foods you are cooking are getting roused up by the activity of the microwaves. When the oven stops or the food is removed, it takes time for the energy to slow down. Cooking continues during that period.

Standing time is a point that most people using microwave ovens forget, ignore, or are not aware of in the first place. Overlooking it spells disaster and disappointment for many who think giving the food "just a few more minutes" will ensure good results. More than likely the food will arrive at the table dry, overcooked, mushy, and sometimes even inedible. Allow for standing time when cooking on your own. The recipes in this book have already provided that in the instructions for you.

WHAT IS ARCING?

Microwaves can be absorbed, reflected, or transmitted, depending on the substance with which they come in contact. Metal containers or containers with any metallic trim, especially gold and silver, reflect the microwaves and cause arcing. You will know it when it happens because it sets off whitish or bluish flashes or sparks that you can see and is accompanied by sharp, crackling sounds that you can hear.

Arcing can ruin your oven since it damages the magnetron tube, which is the heart of the microwave oven. It can also mar cookware and may present a fire hazard. If you see or hear any arcing, stop the oven immediately and find the source of the problem.

Be especially alert when you are using aluminum foil to shield delicate parts of food or the square edges of pans. If there is a small piece of foil touching the side of the oven, arcing will occur. I was especially perplexed one day when I was making rice pudding in what I knew was a special microwave casserole dish. I could see and hear the arcing. I turned the oven on and off several times before I finally noticed that I had not replaced the turntable correctly after the last cleaning, and it was lightly brushing against the side of the oven as it turned!

IS THERE ANY DANGER OF INJURY OR RADIATION?

In a word, the answer is no. All models of microwave ovens have special door seals that are designed to keep microwaves in and prevent leakage. There are also automatic shut-off switches and double and triple interlock systems so that no microwave energy is generated when the door is opened.

It is not necessary to stand away from the door when opening the oven either. Microwaves are tiny, short waves of energy. The energy dissipates very rapidly and follows the inverse square law. This means that the intensity drops as the distance from the source increases.

All microwave manufacturers must adhere to stringent safety standards of the U.S. government and other regulations within the industry. There has never been any known injury from microwave use. Be sure to follow the manufacturers instructions. Always have the oven serviced by a qualified specialist if you find it is not working properly.

WILL MY ELECTRIC BILLS SKYROCKET?

Consumer Reports did an interesting survey comparing the time, cost, and energy of various forms of cooking, using baked potatoes as the reference food item. It was interesting to note that based on national average electricity rates, microwave preparation took less time, used less energy, and cost less than combination or convection cooking and much less than baking in an oven or toaster oven. Today's microwave cooking is speedy, clean, and energy efficient.

An industry survey showed that the majority of microwave users are reheating leftovers, defrosting, baking potatoes, popping corn, and boiling water for drinks. What a pity! For most people it's a lack of understanding and intimidation that keeps them from going further; for others it's a bad experience that discouraged them from trying again.

If you think of microwave cooking as an added dimension to your cooking repertoire, it truly is an adventure. So let's get cooking!

EQUIPMENT

Now that microwave ovens are in virtually every American home, cookware manufacturers have geared up their technology and developed a number of different kinds of materials for microwave cooking. Most of these items can be used in conventional preparation as well, but there are some specifically designed for microwave use only.

Check the package for this information before you purchase new equipment. "Suitable for Microwave," "Microwave-Safe," and "Ideal for Microwave" are some of the industry designations. You can also call the manufacturer to check about items you may already own if there is any question.

In recipes, the terms "microwavable," "micro-proof," and "microwave-safe" are words frequently used by columnists and writers in written recipes. This reminds readers to use proper utensils.

Don't be intimidated and think that you need a lot of fancy gadgets and pans for microwave use. Chances are that you already have casseroles, dishes, and cups that are perfectly suited for microwave cooking. In fact, everyday items like paper plates and paper towels can be used both for cooking and for reheating.

COOKWARE MATERIALS

Microwave cookware is now made in a variety of materials. Some, like permanent plastic, are suitable only for microwave use, while there is no limit on temperature use for products like Corning Ware.

Glass and glass ceramic. These are quite popular and are also the items most people already own. Heat-resistant glass ovenware can be used in either microwave, convection, or conventional ovens at any temperature. Any Pyrex or other ovenproof glass products in good condition are microwavable. Extra care is recommended, however, when using these with high-sugar-content foods where temperatures might rise in excess of 275°F. (This usually occurs in candy making, which, for the most part, is not done in the microwave.) One of the primary advantages of glass is that it is transparent and foods can be seen during and after the cooking process. This can be very helpful in judging when food is done.

Glass ceramic will tolerate any cooking temperature and extremes of temperature, i.e., from freezing to direct, high heat. It is extremely versatile and comes in a wide variety of shapes and sizes; it can be somewhat heavier than other types of materials. Glass ceramic pieces often come with their own lids and covers, which are very handy, especially when preparing soups and casseroles.

Paper. Happily, several types of paper products can be used in the microwave oven. Microwavable paper products are coated with heat-resistant plastic and have primarily been used for single-serving frozen foods. Now available in supermarkets, they represent the ultimate in convenience since they are disposable and clean-up is eliminated altogether. It's useful to know that paper products are meant for short-term use and should be specifically designed for microwave use. These materials include wax paper, plastic-coated paper, and paper towels. Avoid printed and recycled papers which might contain impurities and dyes that could leach into foods. Styrofoam is also not recommended since it can melt if the food inside gets hot enough.

Plastic. Lightweight yet durable, some plastic microwave cookware is made for dual—conventional and microwave—oven use and may be able to withstand temperatures of up to 500°F. Most of these products, however, do level off at about 400°F., so it is important to read the labels and package inserts carefully before using them. Many of these products are attractively designed for cooking and serving, yet also go in the freezer and dishwasher.

Metal. Because microwaves reflect off metal, they can't be absorbed by food and cooking is interrupted. Except for shielding corners of square pans or certain parts of foods, aluminum foil is not recommended for microwave use.

Avoid using metal skewers, dishes, or containers with metal trim, handles, or screws, or wire twist-ties. Whenever any of these materials are used, arcing or sparking may occur. For older model ovens, especially, this could damage the magnetron tube by causing it to heat up. Aluminum may be satisfactory if shallow containers are used and the food quantity is greater than the amount of metal.

Also check that the foil containers are not closer than one inch to the oven walls and don't place them on metal racks when cooking. Finally, it's always best to check the use and care manual and the manufacturer's instructions for the right steps to follow for your model of oven.

COVERS

As in conventional cooking, covers hold in steam and help foods cook faster. A good rule of thumb is that foods that are conventionally cooked with a cover should also be covered in the microwave. Covering encompasses everything from a tight cooking lid to a paper towel or wax paper. Your choice of covering might depend on what you have on hand, and certainly it will always depend on what it is you are preparing at the time. Here are a few easy tips to keep in mind when making the decision.

Most glass, ceramic, and plastic cookware comes with its own matching lid. Some companies make dome covers which can be purchased separately. Adjustable steam vents on these covers provide added versatility. You can also use Pyrex or other ovenproof glass bowls and pie plates as lids. Many dishes, platters, bowls, and plates that you are certain are microwavable make perfect covers.

Paper towels. Paper towels, which are porous, allow steam to escape, and they prevent spatters. They also absorb moisture trapped between food and the floor of the oven. This makes paper towels ideal for reheating breads, muffins, and sandwiches. An added bonus is that they prevent sogginess. Colored towels are not recommended because they may contain oil-based particles that could ignite if dried out. Recycled paper should not be used since it could contain metal fragments that could ignite, causing a fire.

Baked potatoes will be less soggy when wrapped in a paper towel rather than in aluminum foil for their standing time. Burritos rolled this way will not dry out (unless they are overcooked to begin with).

Wet paper towels provide just enough moisture to steam certain foods. Squeeze excess water from paper towels and wrap them around tortillas or crèpes to keep them soft and pliable while heating.

Make steaming bundles for individual servings of vegetables. Place 2 connected paper towels on a flat surface. Lay about 1 cup sliced carrot, broccoli, or cauliflower in the center. Fold in lengthwise toward the center. Fold the ends over toward the center. Put the packet under running water until just moistened (but not soaking wet). Place the packet, folded sides down, on a microwavable plate. Microwave on HIGH for 2 minutes. Let stand for 3 minutes. Split perforation and serve.

Vegetable platters can be steamed with a double layer of wet—but not dripping—paper towels placed over them. This is a nice way to prepare a tray of steamed vegetables, to be served hot or cold, before guests arrive.

Plastic wrap. It is easy to make a tight cover, which holds in more steam and heat, with plastic wrap. Vegetables, fruits, casseroles, stews, and soups are generally prepared covered tightly. But sometimes when cooking temperatures approach 212°F. (the boiling point of water), the plastic wrap shrinks. This can be important if you are cooking foods that contain fats and oils or foods that are cooked for a long time, like dried beans. (In the case of beans, where a really tight cover is desirable, I generally use a casserole that has a cover of its own and add plastic wrap over that to get the best steaming action.)

There are some real distinctions in plastic wraps that you may want to keep in mind. Though most wraps note on the box that they can be used in the microwave, or for microwave reheating, here's what is involved.

Plastic wraps are made of one of three plastic polymers:

• Polyethylene (PE) is used in Glad and Handi-Wrap

• Polyvinyl chloride (PVC) is used in Reynolds plastic wrap

• Polyvinylidene chloride (PVDC) is used in Saran Wrap

It appears that wraps can break down (melt or soften) when subjected to the high temperatures of the microwave oven and leave behind a plasticizer residue which may transfer into foods and could be potentially harmful. The softening temperature of the most popular wraps is 195°F. for PE, 210°F. for PVC, and 250°F. for PDVC.

Close examination of the three types of wraps suggests that some are stronger and safer than others. Evaluations at the laboratories of the Dow Chemical Company show that the best rating is for PVDC film, or Saran Wrap, which has the oxygen protection of glass and is the least likely to melt or shrink during microwave cooking. In addition, the plasticizer used in Saran Wrap is a derivative of citric acid (commonly found in citrus fruits).

It is best to use plastic wraps as covers in such a way that they are not directly in contact with the food being cooked. Place the food in a container or on a plate and draw the wrap across the top so that it is slightly above the food, not touching it.

A "tight" cover is also somewhat of a misnomer, since turning back one corner of the wrap or "venting" is always recommended. This allows a small amount of steam to be released as it is formed. Caution is recommended with tight covers whether they are regular lids or plastic wrap. Always remove them **away** from your face to prevent steam burns.

Wax paper. As a light cover for faster cooking or for reheating without steaming, wax paper is a fine choice. It is also good for preventing splattering and avoids messy cleanups.

Plastic bags. Cooking bags hold in steam. They can be great for cooking mixed vegetables, corn on the cob, and whole or sliced fresh and dried fruits. When using cooking bags, remember to make several slits in the top of the bag. Don't close the bag with metal twist-ties; use nylon ones instead. If these aren't available, cut a ½-inch strip from the open end of the bag to serve as a tie.

Freezer bags. These bags also hold in moisture, but their real value is convenience: They can be used to store, contain, and cook foods. And there isn't any cleanup. Just toss them out when finished. Package leftovers in single portions for easy-to-heat frozen entrees or side dishes. Always remember to pierce the top of the bag to vent before cooking.

If the idea of packaging foods, whether fresh or leftover, appeals to you consider a Seal-a-Meal or other type of home food-packaging system. This accessory wraps and seals food for freezer, refrigerator, or cabinet storage. It eliminates freezer burn and the transfer of odors and humidity. Bags are available in convenient sizes from eight to thirty-two ounces; rolls of plastic film allow you to make the exact size you need.

COOKWARE GUIDELINES

Price, function, size, shape, versatility, durability, and weight are some factors to consider. Here are some tips to consider when selecting microwave cookware:

• Products that can be used for other methods of cooking are the ones to choose. The more ways cookware can be used, the more valuable it is, regardless of the original cost.

• Stacking ability for easy storage is important.

• Lighter weight microwave cookware may be an added attraction, especially if it is to be used by children or the elderly.

• Microwave cookware should resist discoloring and staining and be dishwasher safe. Check package descriptions.

• Cookware should correspond as closely as possible to the shape of the food being prepared, to avoid any excess moisture loss. This is especially important for easy defrosting.

• The preferred cookware shape is round. Very square corners should be avoided, as food may overcook in those areas.

• Ring shapes are most efficient as they allow maximum microwave penetration.

• Specially shaped cookware items include ring or tube shapes for cakes, muffin pans, and racks to raise foods.

• Containers and casseroles should have straight sides and rounded corners to allow for even penetration of the microwave energy.

• Sturdy handles that can be gripped with potholders are important.

• Boil-ups are more frequent in microwaving than in conventional cooking, so allow some extra depth or headroom when choosing cookware.

BEGINNING SET

Several pieces will easily get you started in microwave cooking. Some of the larger dishes will fit only in full-size ovens. Check your oven cavity size before purchasing new items. A basic inventory might include:

• 2-, 4-, and 8-cup Pyrex or other ovenproof glass measuring cups. These are good for liquids, sauces, and soups.

- 1-, 2-, and 3-quart casseroles with lids.

- 2-quart rectangular (11 × 7 inch) or oval baking dishes.

- 9- or 10-inch Pyrex or other ovenproof glass pie plate or cake dish.

- 10- or 12-cup bundt pan.

Take special note of the ovenproof glass measuring cups. These sound like trivial items but they can be most helpful and the most versatile for cooking. In many cases, you will find that they can be used as actual cooking containers; in other cases having a variety of sizes and a few extras make life much easier. You won't have to wash them in between uses or constantly buy odd-size cooking pieces.

ACTIVE ACCESSORIES

Some accessory items are now being called "active." This means that they actively enhance and improve the quality of the food prepared in the microwave oven.

Browning dishes are a popular example of active appliances. Other examples are microwave pressure cookers, micro wafflers, and sandwich grills. Specially designed pizza plates, popcorn poppers, coffee makers, egg cookers, and steamers are also available for microwave use.

TURNTABLES

Many models of microwave ovens come with built-in turntables or carousels. If your oven doesn't have one, I recommend that this be one of your first acquisitions. Turntables help promote more even distribution of the microwaves in the food and thus assure more even cooking and overall better results. But the real bonus is that they eliminate rotating the dish half and quarter turns during cooking. Turntables can also reduce stirring and rearranging foods, but they may not completely eliminate this step. You will want to follow what the recipe method suggests.

These flat, round trays come in a variety of sizes to fit your microwave oven, whether it is a full-size or compact unit. The turntables are usually powered by pressure-activated spring mechanisms; some are battery charged.

BROWNING SKILLETS

It's now a myth that browning is impossible in the microwave oven. Browning trays give food the appetizing, golden appearance of foods cooked in a conventional oven or on top of the stove.

Made of glass ceramic, the dishes are coated on the bottom with a special material that absorbs microwave energy when the empty dish is preheated. The hot surface then browns the outside of the food while the microwave energy cooks the inside.

Browning skillets come in a variety of sizes and shapes. They make it possible to prepare foods like grilled sandwiches, French toast, sautéed and stir-fried vegetables, as well as omelets and scrambled and fried eggs. Covers can come in handy when serving larger dishes like stir-fry vegetables, making the browning dish a single cook-and-serve item.

Remember that when browning dishes are preheated they become very hot. It is especially important to use potholders to protect your hands and trivets for the tabletop when using browning trays.

TIPS AND TECHNIQUES

As with any other method of cooking, there are ways of working with the microwave oven and the foods you are preparing that can make the results much better. Try to forget all the stories you've heard about how certain foods don't cook well in the microwave, or worse yet, how you can't really cook in the microwave. "Heating and defrosting are what the microwave does best," they'll say. "Just don't try to get fancy, or try to make an entire meal." Nothing could be further from the truth.

A lot of the frustration and poor results that people have experienced actually comes from a lack of understanding and probably a lack of experience with this type of cooking. I remember when I first started baking. Though I was an experienced cook, I did little baking until I was in my late twenties. I have to admit I was a bit intimidated at first. I approached the recipes cautiously. I was reluctant to change them at all, and I was unfamiliar with the way things should look at certain stages of preparation. But my greatest lesson was that the numbers on the oven dial often had nothing to do with the temperature inside. The only true way to tell was to own and read an oven thermometer and look at it periodically for any changes.

It's the same with microwave cooking. Knowing some tips and techniques—which have been developed from the trial and error of others—will save you lots of disappointment and can add to your pleasure immensely.

STARTING OUT

Read the use and care manual that comes with your oven. This is often the most overlooked step in microwave use. Learn how to install the oven properly, what voltage or special wiring it may require, and the cooking cycles and special features with which your oven is equipped.

Test for the wattage of your oven if there's any question. Wattage is a measure of the oven's total energy capability or power and it varies from 400 watts in a compact unit to 750 watts in a high-power oven. (Often you may see that a recipe has been tested in a 650 watt oven, for example. This gives you a barometer so you can judge timing if your oven is different.)

The simple test for determining oven wattage is to place a 2-cup glass measure filled with 1 cup of water in the center of the oven. Heat on HIGH for 3 minutes, uncovered. If the water comes to a boil, the oven is 600 watts or more.

STANDING TIME

Standing time, to me, is by far the very most important technique in successful microwave cooking. It is often the most overlooked. In fact, many long-time microwave owners don't know what standing time is or how to utilize it when they prepare even the simplest of foods. I think it's one of the reasons that people give up the notion of cooking in the microwave and resort to only reheating and defrosting.

Recall for a minute the information I gave you earlier about how microwaves cook, that molecules continue vibrating and producing heat for several minutes after the microwaves have passed through the food. That means that microwaved foods continue to cook after they are out of the oven. Standing time may last from one to several minutes depending on the food. Read your manual and recipes carefully for precise standing times. This really will make a tremendous difference and give the best results.

Sometimes a recipe may not mention standing time at all. This is because the time lapsed in getting the dish from the oven to the table to the plate is sufficient. So don't be alarmed if every recipe does not account for standing time. Occasionally, though, you may want to include it on your own, or you may be converting a conventional recipe for microwave use. Just keep in mind that foods needing longer standing times are generally those that are larger in weight or size and have a relatively long cooking time.

Standing time can be done in the oven itself or, as may be specified in the recipe, on a flat heat-resistant surface. Placing a sheet of aluminum foil on the counter will reflect heat on to a dish and can help complete the cooking.

KNOWING THE BASICS

Keep in mind a few principles about size, shape, and placement and your results will be much better. Here's a brief review of the most important points:

Size and shape. Small pieces of foods will cook more quickly than large pieces. Most thin foods like sliced vegetables cook faster than less moist and thicker ones.

Arrangement. Food nearest the outside of the plate or dish cooks first. Always arrange the thickest parts of the food toward the outside. Circular patterns work very well in microwave ovens. Use round cookware when you can and arrange foods of a uniform size, like baked potatoes, in a circular pattern for the most uniform cooking.

Amount. Larger quantities take longer to cook. Keep this in mind when increasing recipes or when cooking, for example, four ears of corn instead of two. Simply put: More food equals more time.

Starting temperature. Very cold or frozen foods will take longer to heat through than ingredients at room temperature. Take this into consideration when estimating cooking time.

Covers. Generally speaking, if you would cover in conventional cooking, cover in microwave cooking. The point of covering is to retain moist heat and prevent evaporation. Microwavable dishes, covers, wax paper, and microwavable plastic wraps and bags are ideal choices. Whatever you are using, and even if you want a tight seal, be sure to vent the cover or wrap. Venting prevents steam build-up that can lead to burns when uncovering and also eliminates the possibility of plastic wraps melting on foods. Always remove covers and wraps **away** from your face to avoid steam burns.

Stirring. The center of the dish receives less microwave energy than the outside so stirring can be very important when cooking foods like stews, casseroles, and vegetables. It is especially critical to sauces, puddings, and egg dishes.

Turning. This usually refers to moving the pan or dish that contains the food while cooking. Again, the idea is to try to get the most even distribution of energy and to help all parts of the food cook evenly. Give the dish a quarter turn halfway through cooking time. Of course this is unnecessary if your oven comes with a built-in carousel. You can also buy a separate turntable (see pages 16–17).

Salt. Always salt after cooking in the microwave, especially vegetables. Salt draws liquid out of food and can actually leave spots on food where dehydration has occurred. This includes seasoned salts like onion salt, garlic salt, and other blends.

Always undercook. This is a wise precept to follow, especially when first using the microwave oven. Use the lower number of minutes when a range of cooking time is given. You can always add a few minutes if something is underdone, but there's nothing more frustrating than going just a bit too far. And remember the principle of standing time: Foods will continue to cook when taken from the microwave to a greater degree than in conventional cooking.

Power levels. Use a lower power setting to avoid overcooking sensitive foods like cheese, eggs, and creamed foods.

Cleaning. See your manual for specific instructions on care and cleaning. Most ovens may be cleaned with a wet paper towel. A general all-purpose cleanser is baking soda. Mix 2 tablespoons baking soda with 2 cups warm water and wipe clean. This also helps keep the interior free from odor. For stubborn stains, sprinkle with dry baking soda and rub lightly with a moist sponge. Do not use scouring pads, commercial chemical oven cleaners, or sharp-edged utensils for cleaning.

TEST YOUR DISHES FOR MICROWAVE USE

Follow the simple experiment at the top of the next page to help you determine if your mugs, dishes, platters, or casseroles are microwavable.

. . . .

1. Place a 1-cup Pyrex or other ovenproof glass measure filled with ½ cup of water in the oven.

2. Put the dish to be tested near but not touching the measure.

3. Close the door and microwave on HIGH for 1 minute.

4. If the dish is cool or slightly warm, it is safe to use in the microwave. The water should be quite warm or hot. If the dish has become hot, don't use it for microwave cooking.

WHAT TO AVOID IN THE MICROWAVE

As much as I dislike the use of "do not," there are truly some things you do not want to do in the microwave oven. Here are the most significant:

• Do not use metal utensils, skewers, plates, dishes, or anything with a metallic trim. This may cause arcing and can damage your oven.

• Do not use wire twist-ties to close cooking bags.

• Do not cook whole eggs in the shell. They will explode, as will unpeeled hard-boiled eggs.

• Do not cook tough-skinned fruits and vegetables like apples, spaghetti squash, acorn squash, etc., whole, unless pricked beforehand with a fork in several spots.

• Do not ever deep-fry in the microwave oven.

• Do not use paper towels unless they are especially made for microwave use. Some paper towels contain synthetic fibers like nylon, which may ignite and lead to fires.

• Do not use mugs or cups with glued handles. Over time the glue can melt and lead to accidents and burns.

• Do not sterilize canning jars in the microwave.

. . . .

- Do not attempt canning in the microwave.

- Do not use conventional food thermometers. Special microwave thermometers are available.

SPECIAL TIPS

The microwave is a great aide in preparing ingredients for later use or performing tasks in less time than it would take using conventional means. Let's look at some of the special ways in which the microwave can be of service.

Blanching almonds. Place 1 cup water in a 4-cup glass measure and microwave on HIGH for 2 to 3 minutes, or until the water boils. Add 1 cup of almonds. Microwave on HIGH for 1 minute. Drain and rub the nuts between 2 pieces of paper towel to remove skin. Spread nuts on paper towels to dry.

Toasting nuts. Spread 1 cup of nuts in a shallow glass dish. Microwave on HIGH for 3 to 4 minutes, or until just browned. Stir several times while toasting. Let stand for 5 minutes before using.

Citrus fruits. Oranges, lemons, and limes will yield more juice when pricked once or twice and microwaved on HIGH for 15 to 20 seconds. Let stand for 1 minute. Roll between your palms several times. If doing several at the same time, place them in a circle when heating.

Drying citrus peel. Make your own dried lemon, lime, or orange peel. Grate the peel and place on a glass dish. Microwave on HIGH for 30 to 45 seconds or until dry and crumbly. Let stand 1 to 2 hours or until completely cooled and brittle. Wrap tightly and store.

Drying coconut. Place ½ cup grated fresh coconut in a thin layer on a microwavable dish. Microwave on HIGH for 2 to 3 minutes, or until golden, stirring each minute or so. Cool and store in an airtight container.

Drying herbs. To keep herbs all year long, place about ½ cup of fresh leaves between paper towels. Microwave on HIGH for 1 to 2 minutes, or until dry and crumbly. Cool and store in an airtight container.

Cutting winter squash. Acorn, butternut, and spaghetti squash cut more easily when lightly preheated. Microwave, uncovered, on HIGH for 1 to 2 minutes. Let stand several minutes before cutting.

Softening underripe avocados. These can be softened for quicker use. Microwave on HIGH for about 1 minute. Let cool completely before cutting. (This technique is best used for guacamole when ripe flavor is less important.)

Croutons. Melt 4 tablespoons of butter or margarine in a 12 x 8-inch microwavable casserole on HIGH for 1 minute. Stir in 4 cups of bread cubes and 1 teaspoon of dried herbs, if desired. Microwave on HIGH for 3 to 5 minutes, uncovered, stirring every 2 minutes or so. The croutons will harden when cool. The butter can also be eliminated, if desired. Crushing croutons in a food processor makes great homemade bread crumbs.

Hot towels. A refreshing start and perfect finale for any meal is a warm moist towel. Use thin washcloths just barely dampened with water. Sprinkle with lime or lemon juice and roll up. Place side by side on a microwavable plate or in a shallow wicker basket. Microwave on HIGH for about 20 seconds per towel.

Now let's look at some hints for reheating, melting, and softening techniques that are so handy in microwave use.

REHEATING

It takes about 2 minutes on HIGH to reheat 1 cup of solid, chilled food. Egg- and cheese-based foods are best reheated on MEDIUM-HIGH.

Coffee, tea, or cider. Cook on HIGH for 1½ to 2 minutes. Let stand several seconds. Add cinnamon stick or a few cloves to cider or tea for special flavor.

Casseroles. Cover with a lid or vented plastic wrap. Cook on HIGH for about 2 minutes per cup of refrigerated food. Stir occasionally and rotate the dish several times if you do not have a turntable. Foods at room temperature need less time. Be sure to allow standing time. Remember that water and fat attract heat and allow even distribution of energy. You may want to add a bit of either, or both, for better results.

Plated room-temperature foods. Arrange foods with thicker, denser items around the outside. When steaming broccoli, for instance, place stalks so that florets are toward the inside and the thicker parts are toward the outside of the plate or casserole. Cover with vented plastic wrap or wax paper. Cook on HIGH for about 2 minutes. The bottom, center portion of the plate should be warm to the touch. Let stand about 30 seconds.

Tortillas and pita breads. These become more pliable and easier to fill when softened first. Loosely wrap in plastic wrap or a paper towel. Microwave on HIGH for 5 to 10 seconds for each one being heated. Let stand several seconds before using.

Snack foods. Foods like pretzels, popcorn, and crackers can be recrisped. Line a wood or straw basket or 1-quart baking dish with paper towels. Microwave 2 to 3 cups on HIGH, uncovered, about 1 minute. Let stand 3 to 4 minutes.

SOFTENING

A number of frequently used foods are quickly softened in the microwave. Here are some of the most common foods with which you will use this technique. Remember to allow a few seconds standing time here just as in regular microwave preparation.

FOOD	AMOUNT	LEVEL	TIME
Butter or margarine	½ cup (1 stick)	MEDIUM	10–15 seconds
Cream cheese	3-ounce package	MEDIUM	1 minute
	8-ounce package	MEDIUM	2 minutes
Ice cream	1 quart	MEDIUM	45 seconds
	½ gallon	MEDIUM	1 minute

FOOD	AMOUNT	LEVEL	TIME
Brown sugar (covered, put in 1 slice apple)	1 cup	HIGH	30 seconds
Crystallized honey or jam (uncovered)	1 cup	HIGH	1 minute
Dried fruit (covered, sprinkled with 1 tablespoon water)	1 cup	HIGH	1 minute
Peanut butter	½ cup	HIGH	30 seconds

MELTING

Using a few seconds more takes softened foods to the melted stage. Here are the foods most frequently melted.

FOOD	AMOUNT	LEVEL	TIME
Butter or margarine	½ cup (1 stick)	HIGH	1 minute
Chocolate (uncovered)			
baking	1-ounce square	MEDIUM	2 minutes
	4 squares	MEDIUM	3–4 minutes
chips	1 cup	MEDIUM	2½–3½ minutes
sweet	4-ounce block	MEDIUM	3–4 minutes
candy bar	1.45-ounce bar	MEDIUM	1–2 minutes

SPECIAL TIPS FOR BAKING

Quick breads don't brown in the microwave as they do in a conventional oven, but a few tricks can greatly enhance their appearance.

• Use whole-grain flours, bran, wheat germ, molasses, maple syrup, brown sugar, cinnamon, and cocoa powder to add a darker, richer color.

• Reduce leavening by about half the original amount. Batters with higher sugar, fat, and egg content produce better breads and muffins.

- Use oils rather than butter or margarine to improve texture. They make finer and lighter products.

- Round or ring pans give the best results, though loaf and square pans can be used.

- Shield corners with triangles of smoothly wrapped aluminum foil to prevent overcooking.

- Sprinkle the pan with graham cracker crumbs, granola, or chopped nuts to enhance appearance.

- Elevate baking pan or dish on a shallow inverted microwavable dish or on a rack. This brings the batter closer to the center of the oven and helps to cook evenly.

- Cook on MEDIUM for initial stage of cooking then finish off at HIGH.

- Check for doneness. When a wooden cake tester or toothpick inserted in the center comes out clean, cake, breads, and muffins are done. It's all right if the top appears slightly moist. Another good sign is when you lightly touch the moist area and it sticks to your finger yet reveals a completely dry cake below.

- Set baked items on a heat-resistant surface to finish cooking. It's necessary to have heat reflected back into breads or muffins. A cooling rack is used only in the final stage, after the bread is turned out of the pan.

DESSERTS

Since sugar and fat attract microwaves, many dessert recipes are very suitable for microwave cooking, if you allow for a few minor changes in the time required.

Crisps and cobblers. These fruit desserts adapt very well to the microwave. They cook in about a third of the conventional time. Whole wheat flour, brown sugar, nuts, and cinnamon give a nice brown top. Place under a regular broiler for a minute after cooking if a crisper top is desired.

Cheesecakes. Cheesecakes are very adaptable to microwave preparation; they turn out deliciously creamy. Heat the filling in a separate bowl on HIGH for a few minutes just to heat through. This helps it to cook more evenly later. Once the filling is poured into the prepared crust, cook on MEDIUM. Place the cheesecake pan on an inverted bowl or rack in the microwave to distribute the heat most evenly. Because of its density, a cheesecake will need a longer standing time to finish cooking. It should be almost set when done. Test with your finger about 1 inch from the center. It should stick to your finger yet still appear moist and set beneath. If the edges are firm or cracked it's been overcooked.

Puddings. Cornstarch or instant tapioca for puddings can be used in equal amounts. Puddings are cooked uncovered to promote thickening. They require stirring during the last half of cooking to avoid lumps. They are done when they begin to boil and are thick and pourable; remember they also thicken upon cooling.

PIES

Crumb- and streusel-topped pies are best, but a double-crust fruit pie can also be prepared in the microwave. Finish it off in a conventional oven for a golden-brown crust.

• Uncooked fillings can be microwaved in a cooked crust.

• Custard fillings do best when they are partially cooked before adding to the crust. Then microwave on MEDIUM to set the custard.

EGGS

U.S. Grade A large eggs were used for recipes in this book. Eggs have a poor reputation in the microwave, and this is most unfortunate as eggs that are handled well will prepare well.

- MEDIUM is the preferred setting for dishes with a high proportion of egg.

- Heating custards before pouring into pie crusts will produce better results.

- Puncture egg yolks lightly to prevent bursting when cooking.

- Hard-boiled eggs in the shell are not recommended. Like hard-skinned vegetables, they can explode.

- Soufflés require some major adaptation to be successful. It's best to wait until you're more experienced with microwave preparation, or use a recipe that's already "tried and true."

CASSEROLES

These types of dishes are well suited for microwave preparation and will require less liquid and fat than conventional methods. For guaranteed success every time:

- Cut foods about the same size and shape for best results.

- Precook some items like hard vegetables and potatoes before combining all ingredients. Note that vegetables are especially slow to soften in tomato sauces; a quick steaming beforehand may help keep textures consistent.

- Stir casseroles several times during cooking to evenly distribute heat.

- Cover with a lid or vented plastic wrap. A good rule of thumb to follow is if you cover in conventional recipe, cover in microwave cooking.

Cooking time depends on the starting temperature of the food. Consider whether casserole ingredients are at room temperature, refrigerated, or frozen and adjust accordingly. Manufacturers' instructions can be most helpful here. Refer to your own power level settings.

SOUPS

Excellent soups of all types can be made in the microwave. Chilled soups such as Strawberry Soup (pages 59–60) develop an even fuller flavor when cooked first.

- Cook on HIGH to bring to a boil.

- Use MEDIUM power setting to simmer soups.

- Choose large, deep casseroles, especially for milk-based soups. These have a tendency to boil up during cooking.

- Stir thickened soups 2 or 3 times to prevent lumping.

- Use a lid or vented plastic wrap if soup is to be simmered for a long time. This will develop flavor and prevent evaporation.

SAUCES

Both sweet and savory sauces work well in the microwave oven. Flour, cornstarch, or tapioca are excellent thickeners.

- Blend all ingredients well.

- Stir 2 to 3 times during cooking.

- Use a 2- or 4-cup glass measure. (A wooden or microwavable plastic spoon can be left in the measure to stir the sauce during cooking for real convenience; it also eliminates sloppy drips.)

SEASONING

There has been a lot of hoopla about whether to increase or decrease certain herbs and spices when cooking in the microwave. I know it certainly had me baffled in my early attempts. Trying to remember what happened with various spices, and when, was very confusing.

The American Spice Trade Association was kind enough to come to my rescue when I brought this dilemma to them as I started writing this book. Their test kitchen worked it through and reported that for the most part, there is no cause for concern here and little, if any, difference in how microwaving affects herbs and spices. The flavors of some highly flavored seasonings like curry and chili powder or crushed red pepper may be intensified slightly. You might want to cut back on these, at least in the beginning, until you've had a chance to experiment a bit.

The most important recommendation was regarding the storage of dried herbs and spices. The Spice Association suggests that spices be kept tightly covered in an airtight container. Don't expose them to extremely high heat or intense light. The bottom line is, don't use stale or poorly stored seasonings.

HOW TO CONVERT A RECIPE FOR MICROWAVE USE

Many of your favorite recipes can be adapted for use in the microwave oven. A few dishes, however, cannot be made well in the microwave or made even similar to recipes prepared in a conventional oven. There are some basic guidelines to follow that will make conversions easier and more successful for you. Here are some tips to help you convert some favorites from your collection:

1. Find a microwave recipe that is similar to the one you want to convert and use it as a guide.

2. Choose microwavable utensils similar in size and shape (i.e., casseroles, baking dishes, lids, etc.). Remember: no metallic trims.

3. Reduce the amount of liquid to about three-fourths of the original recipe.

4. Reduce the amount of fat at least by half and frequently completely. Because of the moist and quick heat of the microwave you can keep the amount of fat at an all-time low with no flavor loss. Baked items, however, do require the same or more fat for tender results.

5. Reduce conventional cooking time by a quarter to a third. Use a similar microwave recipe as a guide. Most important, check for doneness at the early stages until you've had some practice. It's always best to undercook first, then continue to give it a minute or two more.

6. Include standing time in your conversion. This may be one of the most important considerations to include. Depending on the density of the food, allow two to ten minutes standing time to complete the cooking process.

Most manufacturers include cookbooks with microwave ovens, and many of these give instructions for recipe conversion. Invariably they will contain a microwave version for a familiar recipe. Use this as your guide; it will also help you to remember to include techniques like stirring, rotating, and standing.

Some recipes do not convert well, including fried foods, crusty foods like puff pastry and popovers, angel food cakes, and large candy recipes. Yeast breads can be proofed successfully in the microwave but truly need a special formulated recipe. (Some flour manufacturers have begun to make them available. Check the package for recipe offers or call the company's consumer services department.)

HIGH-ALTITUDE MICROWAVING

There are virtually millions of cooks who live in high-altitude areas all over the world. At these higher elevations certain changes affect microwave as well as conventional cooking.

Some adjustments are necessary because the air weighs less and exerts less pressure on everything. Water boils at a lower temperature and liquids evaporate more rapidly than at sea level. Since the atmosphere tends to be drier, baked products tend to be drier. They are also more porous and are more likely to fall during baking. Though you probably won't be doing much baking in your microwave oven, there are a few general guidelines to consider:

• Use larger dishes. Foods tend to expand, foam, and bubble more.

• Increase liquids. Due to evaporation and the lower boiling point of water, an extra 1 to 3 tablespoons of water for vegetables is usually necessary.

- Increase cooking time slightly. Again, due to a lower boiling point, foods do not get as hot. When a range of cooking time is given the maximum amount will generally be required. (Beans and grains certainly will need a longer time to cook.)

- Cover foods, especially during standing and reheating. Hot foods cool faster at higher elevations.

- Use large or jumbo eggs in baked products. They will add more moisture and structure.

- Check with your local utility or public service company. They may have developed specific guidelines for your area.

There is no simple formula for adjusting high-altitude microwave recipes, but keeping these few tips in mind will help you be more pleased with the results.

FOR BEST RESULTS

Whether you're a newcomer to microwave cooking or have already been at it for a while, it's best to keep the following guidelines in mind:

• Measure carefully. All of the recipes were tested using household measuring cups, spoons, and scales. Try to be as accurate as possible to assure the best results.

• Use cookware similar in size and shape to that described in the instructions.

• Use the lower amount of time when a range and test for doneness are given (i.e., microwave on HIGH for 8 to 12 minutes, or until tender-crisp) to get the best results. Individual oven wattage and local power supply may vary, so these guides will help.

• Keep your microwave oven plugged into its own outlet for maximum efficiency and be aware of seasonal brownouts which can affect cooking time.

• The recipes in this book were tested in 650- and 700-watt ovens. If you have a lower wattage oven, add additional time. Usually an increase of about 15 percent will do.

• Note that the power levels indicated in these recipes are based on the percentage equivalents listed below. Check your oven manual to see if they are the same. If they differ, cooking times will change and need to be adjusted accordingly.

HIGH	100%
MEDIUM-HIGH	70%
MEDIUM	50%
MEDIUM-LOW	30%
LOW	10%

SIMPLE STARTERS

Garlicky Steamed Artichokes

Caponata

Crunchy Glazed Nuts

Cumin-roasted Cashews

New Potato Bites

Chilled Vegetable Platter

Scallion Bows with Mustard Sauce

Tortilla Chips

Nachos Supreme

Quesadillas with Salsa Verde

Carrot Soup

Esther's Leek and Potato Soup

Chestnut Soup

Cheddar-Jack Soup

Cucumber Soup

Green and Red Pepper Potato Soup

Potato Quinoa Soup

Hearty Vegetable Soup

Mike's Corn Chowder

Thai Vegetable Soup

Tortilla Soup

Butternut Squash Bisque

Strawberry Soup

Appetizers offer more variety than any other course on the menu. Whether a hearty soup or a platter of steamed vegetables with a light sauce, the simple starters here are a nice way to begin a meal. They're also great for welcoming guests and helping to get folks acquainted.

Personally, I think appetizers are perfect party fare. Sometimes I like to entertain and serve a variety of hot and cold hors d'oeuvres followed by dessert. You may even want to plan an appetizer buffet around an international theme.

If you're looking for a new way to start a meal or want to give a fresh look to gatherings, you'll find these recipes are quick and easy to prepare.

GARLICKY STEAMED ARTICHOKES

Artichokes are so delicious when steamed simply with garlic and parsley that a sauce is unnecessary. Garlic fans will be in their glory with this version; those more timid might prefer to use fewer cloves. Cilantro, oregano, capers, Parmesan cheese, and even a touch of grated ginger can make nice flavor variations. Add your favorites when spreading the leaves and inserting the garlic.

4 medium artichokes (about 6 ounces)
5 large garlic cloves, coarsely chopped
$\frac{1}{2}$ teaspoon freshly ground black pepper
$\frac{1}{2}$ cup chopped parsley, divided
3 tablespoons olive oil
$\frac{1}{4}$ cup water
$\frac{1}{2}$ teaspoon salt

Cut off the stems of the artichokes to be flush with the bottoms. Slice off about 1 inch from the top of the globe. Remove and discard any coarse outer leaves if necessary. Using kitchen shears, snip off any thorny tips, about ¼ inch from the tops of the remaining leaves.

Place the artichokes in a 10-inch round microwavable baking dish or glass pie plate. Spread open the leaves of each artichoke and insert a little of the chopped garlic between each leaf until all the garlic is used up. Sprinkle with pepper and half of the chopped parsley. Drizzle oil over the artichokes. Pour in ¼ cup water and add salt. Cover tightly with vented plastic wrap. Microwave on HIGH for 12 to 16 minutes, or until the bottoms pierce easily with a knife. Rotate the dish every 4 minutes. Let stand, covered, for 5 minutes.

(At this point, the artichokes may be refrigerated and served at a later time, either reheated or at room temperature.) Before serving, drain well, sprinkle with remaining parsley and additional pepper, if desired, and serve.

Makes 4 servings

CAPONATA

This eggplant appetizer makes a wonderful hors d'oeuvre or starter. I generally leave the skin on the eggplant, but peel it if you prefer and just reduce the cooking time a bit. Serve the Caponata with crusty whole wheat Italian bread or grain crackers. Don't worry about leftovers. Reheating Caponata in a sandwich with a slice of mozzarella may be one of the best reasons for making it.

1 eggplant, unpeeled and cut into ½-inch cubes (about 1½ pounds)
⅓ cup olive oil, divided
2 garlic cloves, minced
1 medium onion, thinly sliced
1 celery rib, thinly sliced
1 medium tomato, coarsely chopped
¼ cup oil-cured olives, pitted and chopped
2 tablespoons capers, drained
2 tablespoons balsamic vinegar
1 tablespoon lemon juice
1 teaspoon dried basil
½ teaspoon dried oregano
¼ teaspoon crushed red pepper
Salt and freshly ground black pepper to taste

In a 3-quart microwavable casserole, combine the eggplant and about half of the oil. Cover tightly with a lid or vented plastic wrap. Microwave on HIGH for 3 minutes. Add the remaining oil and toss well to combine. Re-cover and microwave on HIGH for 5 to 7 minutes, or until the eggplant is quite tender. Remove the eggplant with a slotted spoon.

Add the garlic, onion, and celery to the casserole; stir to combine and coat lightly with the oil remaining in the casserole. Cover tightly with a lid or vented plastic wrap. Microwave on HIGH for 3 to 5 minutes, or until the onion is soft.

Return the eggplant to the casserole and add the remaining ingredients; stir well. Cover and microwave on HIGH for 6 to 8 minutes, or until the eggplant and onion are very soft. Rotate the casserole twice during cooking. (Timing will vary,

....

depending on whether or not you have peeled the eggplant and also on how soft you would like it to be.) Let stand, covered, for 5 minutes.

Chill several hours or overnight. Before serving, adjust the seasonings and add additional vinegar and lemon juice if desired.

Makes about 5 cups

CRUNCHY GLAZED NUTS

Guests may not be able to stop nibbling on these sweet and spicy nuts. They have been a hit at all of my gatherings. Make several batches and store them in an airtight container.

....

1 egg white, lightly beaten
2 cups walnut or pecan halves
¼ cup packed brown sugar
½ teaspoon ground ginger
¼ teaspoon ground cinnamon
¼ teaspoon ground red pepper

....

In a 10-inch glass pie plate, combine the egg white and nuts, tossing until the nuts are moistened. In a small bowl, combine the remaining ingredients. Sprinkle over the nuts and toss well until they are completely coated. Spread out in a single layer. Microwave on HIGH, uncovered, for 4 to 6 minutes, or until the nuts are heated through and the glaze is bubbling, stirring every 2 minutes. (The nuts will crisp as they cool.) Stir again after removing from the oven.

Let cool in the pie plate for about 15 minutes. Using a spatula, stir to remove any nuts on the sides and bottom of the plate. Gently separate any that are stuck together.

Serve or store in an airtight container.

Makes 2 cups

....

CUMIN-ROASTED CASHEWS

Here's another version of nuts that makes a fine party snack. The cumin adds a Mexican flavor, making them good to serve with beer.

4 tablespoons butter or margarine
2 cups cashews
1½ teaspoons Tabasco sauce
½ teaspoon ground cumin
¼ teaspoon salt

Place the butter in a 10-inch glass pie plate. Microwave on HIGH for 1 minute or until the butter is melted. Stir in remaining ingredients and toss well until the nuts are coated. Spread out in a single layer. Microwave on HIGH, uncovered, for 4 to 6 minutes, or until the nuts are heated through, stirring every 2 minutes. Stir again after removing from the oven. Cool nuts in the pie plate for about 15 minutes.

   Serve or store in an airtight container.

Makes 2 cups

NEW POTATO BITES

Potatoes are always popular. These red nuggets are especially tasty and can be quite low in calories when yogurt, mustard, or salsa are the accompaniments.

12 new potatoes, about 2 inches in diameter
Toppings and garnishes (see right)

Pierce the potatoes with a fork. Place on a double layer of paper towels in a circle on the floor of the oven. Microwave on HIGH for 8 to 11 minutes, or until tender, rearranging and turning once during cooking. Let stand for 5 minutes.

Cut potatoes in half. Scoop out about a teaspoon of the flesh, using a small spoon or melon baller. Arrange the potato shells on a serving platter, fill with any of the suggested toppings, and garnish with herbs.

Makes 4 to 6 servings

Toppings: Yogurt, sour cream, Roquefort cheese, capers, red or green salsa, guacamole or coarse-grain mustard, toasted sesame or sunflower seeds
Garnishes: Chopped parsley, cilantro, and chives

CHILLED VEGETABLE PLATTER

A pretty and most appealing starter is a platter of fresh, lightly steamed vegetables. Vary the vegetables but remember that arrangement is the secret to microwaving several foods with different cooking times. Cover with a light vinaigrette before serving or pass Yogurt-Cucumber Dressing at the table.

1 pound slender asparagus, trimmed
6 medium mushrooms (about 4 ounces)
½ pound yellow squash, cut into ½-inch slices
1 medium zucchini (about 6 ounces), cut into 2½ x ¼-inch strips
1 medium carrot, cut into 2½ x ¼-inch strips
1 small red bell pepper, cored, seeded, and sliced into thin rings
2 tablespoons water
2 cups Yogurt-Cucumber Dressing (page 211)

Arrange the asparagus spears in the center of a 12- to 14-inch round microwavable platter. Arrange mushrooms, squash, zucchini, and carrots around the spears, alternating colors and types of vegetables; place red pepper rings over the top. Sprinkle with water and cover with vented plastic wrap. Microwave on HIGH for 6 to 9 minutes, or until tender-crisp, rotating the platter twice during cooking. Feel through the wrap to test for doneness; vegetables should feel soft to the touch and pliable. Let stand, covered, for 5 minutes.

Makes 6 to 8 servings

SCALLION BOWS WITH MUSTARD SAUCE

Steamed scallions tie up into attractive and tasty appetizers. Choose slender scallions uniform in size.

16 scallions
¼ cup water or vegetable stock
½ cup Mustard Sauce (page 210)

Rinse the scallions, trim roots, and cut off green tops so that the scallions measure about 5 inches.

Arrange on a 12-inch round microwavable platter with the white part of the scallions on the outside of the plate. Cover tightly with vented plastic wrap. Microwave on HIGH for 3 minutes, or until the green ends are limp, then immediately plunge into cold water. Remove any outside layer of scallion bulb. Cool and blot dry.

Loosely tie each scallion so that there is a knot in the center. Place on a lacquered tray or serving platter.

Serve with a small bowl of Mustard Sauce.

Makes 4 servings

TORTILLA CHIPS

Guests will swoon when you bring out warm chips almost devoid of extra oil and salt. Use corn, flour, or whole wheat tortillas and be sure to make lots—they disappear fast.

1 to 2 tablespoons canola or vegetable oil
6 tortillas, 6 inches in diameter

Lightly brush both sides of the tortillas with oil, then cut each tortilla into 6 triangles. Lay the triangles in a single layer in a 9 × 11-inch microwavable dish or on a flat plate. Microwave on HIGH for 2 to 3 minutes, or until the chips are crisp and lightly browned, turning once. Cool.

To reheat, place chips in a wicker basket or dish lined with a paper towel; microwave on HIGH for 30 seconds.

Makes 2 cups

NACHOS SUPREME

There's no faster or easier way to make nachos than in the microwave. The combination of beans and cheese here is a good source of protein and calcium. You can substitute the salsa verde on page 46 for the pickled jalapeño slices.

1 16-ounce can vegetarian refried beans (2 cups)
4 cups Tortilla Chips (pages 44–45)
1 cup shredded Monterey Jack cheese (4 ounces)
1 cup shredded Cheddar cheese (4 ounces)
½ cup sliced pitted black olives
¼ cup pickled jalapeño pepper slices, drained
¼ cup thinly sliced scallions

Place the refried beans in a medium microwavable bowl. Microwave on HIGH for 2 minutes. Stir and set aside.

Arrange the chips on a 12-inch round glass platter. Sprinkle about half of each cheese over the chips. Spoon dollops of refried beans on top. Sprinkle with the remaining cheese, the olives, and pepper slices. Microwave on MEDIUM-HIGH for 3 minutes, or until the cheese is melted.

Sprinkle with scallions and serve.

Makes 6 servings

QUESADILLAS WITH SALSA VERDE

If there's time, prepare the salsa the night before to let the flavor blend. I use the seeds of the jalapeño pepper, and this recipe renders a medium-hot version. Add more or less of the seeds as you prefer. The green salsa is most refreshing, and a nice change from the usual red sauce.

1 pound tomatillos, husked and washed, or 1¾ cups canned
   tomatoes, drained
¼ cup coarsely chopped red onion
2 tablespoons lime juice
6 cilantro sprigs
1 medium jalapeño pepper, quartered
1 medium onion, thinly sliced
1 tablespoon olive oil
2 cups grated Monterey Jack cheese (8 ounces)
1 teaspoon dried oregano
½ teaspoon ground cumin
6 flour tortillas, 7 inches in diameter

Core and quarter the tomatillos if using fresh one. Place the tomatillos, onion, lime juice, cilantro and pepper in a food processor or blender. Process for about 30 seconds, or until the salsa is combined and still a bit chunky. Pour into a small bowl or serving dish. Cover and refrigerate.

In a 1-quart microwavable casserole, combine the onion and oil. Cover tightly with lid or vented plastic wrap. Microwave on HIGH for 4 to 6 minutes, or until onion is very tender and translucent, stirring once. Let cool.

Stir in the cheese, oregano, and cumin until combined. Place a tortilla on a paper towel on a large microwavable plate. Top with a heaping half cup of the cheese mixture, leaving a ¼-inch border around the outside. Lay another tortilla on top. Microwave on MEDIUM-HIGH for 2 minutes, or until the cheese is melted. Let stand for several seconds. Repeat with the remaining tortillas.

Cut each tortilla into quarters and arrange on a platter. Place a heaping teaspoon of salsa on each piece or pass sauce separately.

Makes 2 cups sauce, 12 wedges

CARROT SOUP

Orange juice and ginger give a nice lift to this versatile soup. It was intended to be served hot, but when I brought some of it for friends to try, they served it chilled, and the raves were a surprise. It is full of complex flavor and is very refreshing, not to mention that it is a rich source of vitamins A and C.

2 tablespoons butter or margarine
1 medium onion, chopped
2 pounds carrots, peeled and cut into ¼-inch slices
1 cup chopped celeriac (optional)
1½ teaspoons ginger, minced
3 cups Basic Vegetable Stock (page 199)
1 cup orange juice
1 cup milk or half-and-half
1 teaspoon grated orange peel, orange part only
¼ teaspoon ground nutmeg
¼ teaspoon freshly ground white pepper
Salt to taste
⅓ cup chopped pistachio nuts, for garnish

Place the butter, onion, carrots, celeriac, if using, ginger, and 1 cup of the stock in a 3-quart microwavable casserole. Cover with a lid or vented plastic wrap. Microwave on HIGH for 10 to 14 minutes, or until the carrots are tender, stirring once. Cool slightly.

Puree the carrot mixture in a food processor or blender, gradually adding the remainder of the stock until smooth, and return to the casserole. Slowly stir in the orange juice, milk, orange peel, nutmeg, and white pepper.

Re-cover and microwave on HIGH for 4 to 8 minutes, or until the soup is heated through. Let stand, covered, for 3 minutes.

Adjust the seasonings, adding salt, if desired. Garnish each serving with some pistachio nuts.

Makes 6 servings

ESTHER'S LEEK AND POTATO SOUP

You may think there's cream in this soup even though there isn't a drop. Baking potatoes add a nice richness that doesn't require any enhancement. Esther Plotner, a fellow registered dietitian, does suggest trading some of the stock for milk now and again for an extra boost of calcium. This is especially important for kids and moms-to-be.

2 medium leeks, white parts only, thoroughly washed and thinly sliced (about 1 pound)
1 tablespoon canola oil
2 medium baking potatoes, peeled and cut into 1-inch cubes (about 1 pound)
4 cups Basic Vegetable Stock (page 199) or water
1 cup tightly packed watercress leaves
Salt and freshly ground white pepper to taste
Watercress, for garnish

In a 2-quart microwavable casserole, combine the leeks and oil. Cover with a lid or vented plastic wrap. Microwave on HIGH for 3 minutes. Add the potatoes and stock. Re-cover and microwave on HIGH for 12 to 15 minutes, or until the potatoes are tender.

Stir in the watercress leaves. Re-cover and microwave on MEDIUM for 7 minutes. Cool slightly.

In a food processor or blender, puree the soup in batches until smooth and creamy. Return the soup to the casserole. Adjust seasoning, adding salt and pepper to taste.

Re-cover and microwave on HIGH for 3 to 5 minutes, or until the soup is heated through.

Ladle into soup bowls and garnish with watercress.

Makes 4 servings

CHESTNUT SOUP

Make this soup part of a Thanksgiving meal, perhaps accompanied by winter squash, yams, and a mushroom rice pilaf. The Pumpkin Cheesecake Pie (pages 185–186) for dessert makes a complete and festive vegetarian meal.

4 tablespoons butter or margarine
1 small onion, chopped
4 cups Basic Vegetable Stock (page 199)
1 8-ounce jar unsweetened whole chestnuts, cut in half, or 12 fresh chestnuts, cooked and peeled (see Note)
¼ cup dry sherry
¼ teaspoon ground nutmeg, plus additional for garnish
⅛ teaspoon ground red pepper
1 cup half-and-half

In a 3-quart microwavable casserole, combine the butter and onion. Microwave on HIGH for 2 to 3 minutes, or until the onion is tender. Stir in the stock and chestnuts. Cover tightly with a lid or vented plastic wrap. Microwave on HIGH for 8 to 10 minutes, or until boiling. Stir in the sherry, nutmeg, and pepper and re-cover. Microwave on MEDIUM for 15 minutes. Cool slightly.

With a slotted spoon, remove the chestnuts and onions to a food processor or blender and puree until smooth. With the motor running, slowly pour in stock. Return the soup to the casserole and stir in half-and-half. Re-cover and microwave on MEDIUM for 4 to 6 minutes, or until heated through.

Serve immediately, garnished with a dash of nutmeg.

Makes 4 to 6 servings

NOTE: To cook 12 chestnuts, use a sharp knife to cut an X into the flat side of each one. Place the nuts in a shallow microwavable baking dish. Microwave, uncovered, on HIGH for 4 to 6 minutes, or until the nuts are soft when squeezed, stirring twice. Let stand for 5 minutes and peel. Return peeled chestnuts to the baking dish and microwave for 4 to 6 minutes, or until tender.

CHEDDAR-JACK SOUP

Combining Cheddar and Monterey Jack cheeses with a small apple makes for a very pleasing soup and a rich source of calcium. A hot chili pepper gives it a Southwestern touch. Use the flour if you like a very thick soup, but most times I do without. I especially like to serve this soup in a large round crusty Italian or black bread that has been hollowed out to make a soup tureen.

3 tablespoons butter or margarine
2 medium leeks, white parts only, washed thoroughly and finely sliced
1 medium Golden Delicious apple, peeled, cored, and chopped
1 jalapeño pepper, finely chopped
3 tablespoons unbleached white flour (optional)
3 cups Basic Vegetable Stock (page 199)
1 cup milk or half-and-half
¼ cup white wine (optional)
½ teaspoon dry mustard
1 cup shredded Cheddar cheese (4 ounces)
1 cup shredded Monterey Jack cheese (4 ounces)
1 medium tomato, peeled, seeded, and diced

Place the butter in a 3-quart microwavable casserole. Microwave on HIGH for 1 minute, or is melted. Add the leeks, apple, and jalapeño pepper and stir well to coat with the butter. Microwave on HIGH for 4 to 6 minutes, or until the apple softens, stirring once. Let stand, covered, for 2 minutes to cool.

Transfer the mixture to a food processor or blender. Add 1 cup stock and puree. Return mixture to the casserole. Add flour, if desired, blending well. Stir in remaining stock, milk, white wine, if desired, and mustard. Microwave on HIGH for 4 to 6 minutes, stirring once. Be sure soup doesn't boil. Stir in the cheeses. Microwave on MEDIUM for 4 to 6 minutes, or until the soup is heated through.

To serve, ladle the soup into bowls. Top with some chopped tomato in the center of each. If using bread as a tureen, pour in the soup and spoon about a tablespoon of tomatoes in the center. Pass the remainder of the tomatoes at the table.

Makes 4 to 6 servings

CUCUMBER SOUP

Many cucumber soup recipes are prepared by combining the raw ingredients in a blender, but cooking really enhances the flavor. Since microwaving is the coolest way to cook, you can reap the benefits of cooking even in the heat of summer. This soup is very refreshing and has fewer than 100 calories per serving.

3 medium cucumbers, peeled, seeded, and cut into ¼-inch pieces, divided
3 scallions, white parts with about 1 inch of green parts, thinly sliced
1 tablespoon peanut oil
1 cup Basic Vegetable Stock (page 199)
2 tablespoons white wine
2 cups yogurt or buttermilk
2 tablespoons chopped dill
Salt to taste
Dill sprigs, for garnish

In a 2-quart microwavable casserole, combine all but 1 cup of the cucumbers, the scallions, and oil. Cover tightly with a lid or vented plastic wrap. Microwave on HIGH for 8 to 10 minutes, or until tender, stirring once during cooking. Stir in stock and wine. Cover tightly with a lid or vented plastic wrap. Microwave on MEDIUM for 15 minutes. Cool slightly.

Puree in a food processor or blender until smooth. Return mixture to the casserole. Whisk in yogurt, dill, and salt to taste. Cover and chill for several hours.

Ladle into chilled soup bowls. Garnish with reserved cucumber and a sprig of dill.

Makes 6 servings

GREEN AND RED PEPPER POTATO SOUP

This soup actually is made in two batches; one batch uses green pepper, the other uses red. It's worth the extra effort when you see the beautiful and distinct colors poured into the same bowl. The potato adds extra body and richness to the soup while the lowfat milk keeps the calories low and the nutrition high.

1 tablespoon olive oil
1 garlic clove, minced
¼ cup water
1 large russet potato, peeled and cut into 1-inch cubes
1 cup low-fat milk
½ cup canned roasted green Anaheim chilies
½ teaspoon salt
¼ teaspoon freshly ground white pepper
¼ teaspoon dried thyme
Red Pepper Soup (see right)
Chopped chives, for garnish

In 2-quart microwavable casserole, combine oil and garlic. Microwave on HIGH for 40 seconds. Add the water and potato. Cover tightly with a lid or vented plastic wrap. Microwave on HIGH for 5 to 6 minutes, or until tender. Transfer potatoes, garlic, and cooking liquid to food processor or blender. Return to the casserole and re-cover. Microwave on HIGH for 2 to 3 minutes, or until heated through but not boiling.

Before serving, pour each of the soups into separate 2-cup glass measures. Add milk, chilies, salt, pepper, and thyme. Puree until smooth. Place both cups in the oven together. Microwave on HIGH for 2 to 6 minutes, or until heated through but not boiling. Prepare Red Pepper Soup as directed on the next page.

To serve, pour about ½ cup of each soup into individual bowls simultaneously from opposite sides. The soup will meet in the center. Garnish with chives.

Makes 4 servings

••

Red Pepper Soup: Follow the instructions on the previous page, substituting ½ cup roasted and peeled red peppers or pimientos for the green chilies and ⅛ teaspoon ground red pepper for the thyme.

POTATO QUINOA SOUP

Rosanne Wernick, a vegetarian chef in New York City, developed this recipe. The soup becomes quite thick as it stands. Remember that quinoa is a grain with an exceptional protein profile.

••

2 tablespoons olive oil
1 cup coarsely chopped onion
½ cup coarsely chopped celery
½ cup coarsely chopped carrots
1 tablespoon minced garlic
2 cups shredded cabbage leaves
1 cup unpeeled potatoes, cut into ½-inch cubes
¼ cup quinoa
8 cups water
Salt and freshly ground black pepper to taste
Chopped cilantro, for garnish

••

In a 5-quart microwavable casserole, combine oil, onion, celery, carrots, and garlic. Cover tightly with a lid or vented plastic wrap. Microwave on HIGH for 4 to 5 minutes, or until the carrots are tender.

Add the cabbage and potatoes, stirring well to coat lightly with oil. Add the quinoa and water. Re-cover and microwave on HIGH for 8 to 10 minutes, or until just boiling; stir and add pepper and salt to taste. Re-cover and microwave on MEDIUM for 5 to 8 minutes, or until the potatoes are cooked.

Ladle into soup bowls and garnish with chopped cilantro.

Makes 4 to 6 servings

••

HEARTY VEGETABLE SOUP

I like to make this soup in large batches because it freezes so well. It's also an easy dinner when you're having lots of people over. The Multigrain Mix adds a nice change to a familiar dish. Cooked kidney beans complete the protein and a variety of vegetables round out the color and the flavor. The soup thickens considerably on standing but it takes well to additional water or stock for reheating. Sometimes I leave it thick and pour it over pasta as a sauce.

1 large onion, coarsely chopped (about 2 cups)
2 medium carrots, coarsely chopped (about 2 cups)
2 celery ribs, with leaves, coarsely chopped
2 tablespoons olive oil
1 28-ounce can whole tomatoes, with juices (1¾ cups)
4 cups water or Basic Vegetable Stock (page 199)
¾ cup Multigrain Mix (page 229) or any grain such as rice or barley
1 bay leaf
1 cup sliced mushrooms
1 cup trimmed and sliced green beans
1 cup cooked or canned kidney beans, drained
½ cup chopped parsley
1 tablespoon chopped basil or 1 teaspoon dried basil
1 teaspoon chopped rosemary or ½ teaspoon dried rosemary
¼ teaspoon crushed red pepper

In a 5-quart microwavable casserole, combine the onion, carrots, celery, and oil. Cover tightly with a lid or vented plastic wrap. Microwave on HIGH for 4 minutes. Stir in the tomatoes, breaking them up with the back of a spoon, and add the water or stock, grain mix, and bay leaf. Cover and microwave on HIGH for 12 to 14 minutes, or until boiling. Reduce the setting to MEDIUM-HIGH and cook for 15 minutes.

Stir in the mushrooms, green beans, kidney beans, parsley, basil, rosemary, and red pepper. Re-cover and microwave on MEDIUM-HIGH for 18 minutes, or until the vegetables are tender and the grains are almost tender (remember they will continue to cook and soften somewhat on standing). Let stand, covered, for 10 minutes. Check the consistency and add additional water or stock if desired.

Makes 8 servings

MIKE'S CORN CHOWDER

Corn is my friend Mike Center's favorite food and soups are his favorite dishes to prepare. I know you'll enjoy his corn chowder. You will also be glad to know that milk and corn are a felicitious combination. Milk is rich in lysine and tryptophan, which complement the protein in corn.

· ·

4 cups Tomato Vegetable Stock (page 200)
4 ears corn, kernels removed, or 4 cups drained canned corn
¾ teaspoon salt
1½ cups half-and-half or milk
4 tablespoons unsalted butter
¼ teaspoon crushed red pepper, or to taste
½ roasted red bell pepper, seeded and finely chopped

· ·

In a 3-quart microwavable casserole, combine the stock, corn, and salt. Cover tightly with a lid or vented plastic wrap. Microwave on HIGH for 15 minutes. Cool slightly.

Transfer about three-fourths of the corn mixture to a food processor or blender and puree. Return the puree to the casserole and stir in the half-and-half, butter, and crushed red pepper. Re-cover and microwave on HIGH for 8 to 10 minutes, or until just boiling.

Ladle soup into bowls and garnish with chopped pepper.

Makes 6 servings

· ·

THAI VEGETABLE SOUP

Seitan is a nutrition powerhouse. An excellent source of protein, it contains no saturated fat or cholesterol. Look for marinated seitan in the refrigerated section of your health-food store. Firm tofu can also be used. If your dietary preferences permit, use a bit of nam pla (fish sauce) or stir in soy sauce to round out the flavors.

8 cups Basic Vegetable Stock or Mushroom Stock (pages 199 and 201)
3 stalks fresh lemon grass, tough outer leaves removed and
  cut into 2-inch pieces (see Note)
2 quarter-size pieces fresh ginger
2 to 3 serrano chilies, cut lengthwise into thin strips
1½ teaspoons sweet paprika
6 ounces fresh broccoli
2 cups thinly sliced carrots, cut on a wide diagonal
1 cup shredded (about 1-inch strips) Napa cabbage
8 ounces marinated seitan or firm tofu, drained and cut into ½-inch cubes
1 6¾-ounce can or one 7-ounce jar straw mushrooms, drained (⅔ cup)
Nam pla or soy sauce to taste

Pour the stock through a sieve or strainer lined with a double layer of cheesecloth into a 3-quart microwavable casserole. Add the lemon grass, ginger, chilies and paprika. Cover tightly with a lid or vented plastic wrap. Microwave on HIGH for 10 to 15 minutes, or until boiling. Reduce setting to MEDIUM and microwave another 10 minutes. Cut the broccoli into small florets about 1½ × 1 inch (you should have about 1 heaping cup); set aside. Peel and trim the stalks, cutting them into 1½ × ½-inch sticks (you should have about 1 cup).

    Add the broccoli stems and carrots to the stock. Re-cover and microwave on HIGH for 7 minutes. Stir in the broccoli, cabbage, seitan or tofu, and mushrooms. Re-cover and microwave on HIGH for 5 to 7 minutes, or until the vegetables are tender. Let stand for 5 minutes. Add nam pla or soy sauce to taste.

Makes 4 servings

N O T E : Fresh lemon grass is available at Asian markets.

TORTILLA SOUP

My sister was the one who first ordered this zesty soup at the Hotel Palmilla in Cabo San Lucas at the top of Mexico's Baja California. Light and flavorful, the soup is topped with thin crispy tortilla strips. Though they had been fried at the hotel, I think you'll find this microwave method provides the crunch—without the fat.

4 corn tortillas, cut into ½-inch strips
2 tablespoons olive oil
1 garlic clove, minced
1 cup finely chopped carrots
1 small onion, thinly sliced
4 cups Basic Vegetable Stock (page 199)
1 medium tomato, peeled and diced
2 tablespoons canned chilies, undrained
1 teaspoon chili powder
½ teaspoon ground cumin
½ teaspoon dried oregano
Salt and freshly ground black pepper to taste
Chopped cilantro, for garnish

Place the tortilla strips on a paper towel on the floor of the oven. Microwave on HIGH for 7 minutes, turning once. Transfer to a baking rack and let stand for 1 hour, or until dry and crispy.

In a 2-quart microwavable casserole, combine the oil, garlic, carrots, and onion. Microwave on HIGH for 2 minutes. Stir in stock, tomato, chilies, chili powder, cumin, and oregano. Cover tightly with a lid or vented plastic wrap. Microwave on HIGH for 5 to 7 minutes, or until the soup boils. Microwave on MEDIUM for 10 minutes. Season with salt, if desired, and pepper to taste. To serve, place a handful of tortilla strips in each bowl, fill with soup and garnish with cilantro.

Makes 4 servings

BUTTERNUT SQUASH BISQUE

You'll never suspect that there's no milk or cream in this rich and complex-flavored soup. Sweet potato lends color and thickness. Though it's low in calories, this bisque is loaded with vitamin A.

2 medium butternut or acorn squash (about 1½ pounds each)
1 medium sweet potato (about 8 ounces)
2 tablespoons canola oil
1 cup thinly sliced leeks, white parts only
3 cups Basic Vegetable Stock (page 199)
2 cups water
2 tablespoons dark rum
2 tablespoons lime juice
1 teaspoon salt, or to taste
Ground mace and chopped chives, for garnish
Yogurt or sour cream (optional)

Pierce each squash and the potato several times with the tip of a sharp knife. Place them on a double layer of paper towels in a circle on the floor of the oven. Microwave on HIGH for 8 minutes. Turn each vegetable and microwave on HIGH for 7 to 9 minutes, or until the squash are soft. Set aside and let cool. Depending on the shape of the potato it may be done before or after the squash. Check the potato for doneness and wrap it in a paper towel; set aside. (A fork or knife will pierce the potato easily to the center when done. Otherwise, microwave it on HIGH for another 2 to 4 minutes until done.)

In a 3-quart microwavable casserole, combine the oil and leeks. Cover tightly with a lid or vented plastic wrap. Microwave on HIGH for 3 to 5 minutes, or until the leeks are very tender.

When the squash is cool enough to handle easily, cut in half and scoop out the seeds; set aside. Peel the sweet potato and cut into chunks.

Working in batches in a food processor or blender, puree the squash, potato, and leeks with the stock and water until smooth and creamy. Return the soup to the casserole. Stir in the rum, lime juice, and salt. Cover tightly with a lid or vented plastic wrap. Microwave on HIGH for 8 to 10 minutes, or until heated through, stirring once.

Ladle into soup bowls. Sprinkle with mace and chives. Pass a bowl of yogurt or sour cream at the table, if desired.

Makes 4 to 6 servings

STRAWBERRY SOUP

Fruit soups are usually extremely easy and fast to prepare, never more so than in the microwave. Accolades for this soup go to Felipe Rojas-Lombardi, executive chef and owner of the Ballroom restaurant in New York City, and to his able assistant Rosemarie. Use ripe or slightly overripe berries, without bruises; they have a more pronounced bouquet and produce a sweeter and a more flavorful soup. This soup is pure vitamin C. It is also so low in calories that you may want to splurge with crème fraîche at the end; otherwise use yogurt as suggested. The soup can also be served cold. Stir in the Calvados after pureeing and chill for several hours. Adjust seasonings at this point and proceed with the final steps.

4 pounds fresh strawberries
2 cinnamon sticks (2 inches each)
1 small dried hot red chili pepper
1 quarter-size piece fresh ginger, peeled
⅓ cup sugar
1 tablespoon Calvados, Cointreau, or Triple Sec
2 tablespoons crème fraîche or yogurt (optional)
Crème fraîche or yogurt and mint leaves, for garnish

Briefly rinse the strawberries under cold running water; drain thoroughly. Hull the berries, reserving about 6 of the largest and ripest for a garnish, and cut each into 4 to 6 pieces, depending on the size.

(continued)

(continued)

In a 5-quart microwavable casserole, combine the strawberries, cinnamon, pepper, ginger, and sugar. Cover with a lid or vented plastic wrap. Microwave on HIGH for 12 to 14 minutes, or until just boiling, stirring once. Partially re-cover and microwave on MEDIUM for another 15 minutes, stirring once. Cool slightly.

With a slotted spoon, remove the cinnamon, pepper, and ginger. Working in batches in a food processor or blender, puree the berry mixture until smooth. Return the soup to the casserole and stir in the Calvados. Cover tightly with a lid or vented plastic wrap. Microwave on HIGH for 5 to 7 minutes, or until the soup is heated through.

Adjust the seasonings, adding more sugar if necessary. Stir in the reserved strawberry pieces, and crème fraîche or yogurt, if using.

Ladle into soup bowls. Garnish with a dollop of crème fraîche or yogurt and mint leaves.

Makes 4 servings

SANDWICHES, BREADS, AND SUCH

Black Bean Burritos
Pepper and Onion Hero
Yummy Yam Sandwich
Spinach Melt
Garlic Bread
Hot Cheesy French Rolls
Spicy Corn Bread
Sesame Cream Biscuits
Rosemary-scented Spoon Bread
Good Earth Sandwich
Mini Muffin Pizzas
Five-Minute Mexican Pizza

If you're stuck for a new luncheon idea or tired of the same boring sandwiches, you'll find some nice alternatives here.

Made with a bit of onion and a touch of nutmeg, the Spinach Melt will please everyone at the table. Most folks are accustomed to yams as a side dish; in the Yummy Yam Sandwich they take on a new personality when combined with color and creaminess of the fresh tomato and melted Provolone cheese. Avocado lovers are sure to enjoy the Good Earth Sandwich for a quick lunch or light dinner.

What's best about all of these recipes is that they take so little time to prepare.

BLACK BEAN BURRITOS

A great made-in-advance "sandwich," the burrito has become a popular item. The bean mixture can be made several days in advance to develop more flavor.

1 tablespoon vegetable oil
1 small onion, finely diced
1 jalapeño pepper, seeded and chopped
1 garlic clove, minced
4 tablespoons chopped cilantro, divided
1 teaspoon chili powder
¼ teaspoon ground cumin
2 cups cooked black beans
2 tablespoons water
Salt and freshly ground black pepper to taste
½ avocado, pitted, peeled, and chopped
1 medium tomato, diced
2 scallions, finely chopped
1 tablespoon lemon juice
4 flour tortillas, warmed (page 26)
Garnishes (see below)

In a 1-quart microwavable bowl, stir the oil, onion, pepper, and garlic together. Cover tightly with vented plastic wrap and microwave on HIGH for 2 minutes. Stir in half of the cilantro, the chili powder, cumin, beans, and water. Re-cover and microwave on HIGH for 2 minutes. Season with salt and pepper to taste.

To make the salsa, in a small bowl combine the avocado, tomato, scallions, remaining cilantro, and lemon juice; set aside.

Spread the bean mixture over each tortilla; fold in the sides and roll up to make the burritos. Place on a microwavable platter and cover with vented plastic wrap. Microwave on HIGH for 2 minutes. Serve with salsa and garnishes.

Makes 4 burritos

Garnishes: Shredded lettuce, chopped red onion, grated Monterey Jack or Cheddar cheese, and sour cream

PEPPER AND ONION HERO

I sometimes put a slice or two of mozzarella cheese in this hero, then wrap it in a paper towel and heat it on HIGH for one minute. Peppers are a rich source of vitamin C and carotenoids, which the body converts to vitamin A.

1 large green bell pepper, seeded and cut into 1 × ½-inch strips
1 large red bell pepper, seeded and cut into 1 × ½-inch strips
1 large onion, thinly sliced
¼ cup oil-cured olives, pitted and finely chopped
2 tablespoons extra-virgin olive oil
½ teaspoon dried thyme
1 small loaf Italian bread

In a 3-quart microwavable casserole, combine the peppers, onion, olives, oil, and thyme. Cover tightly with a lid or vented plastic wrap. Microwave on HIGH for 6 minutes, stirring once. Let stand, covered, for 2 minutes. Slice bread in half lengthwise, then spoon the pepper mixture inside. Cut loaf in half and serve.

Makes 2 servings

YUMMY YAM SANDWICH

Use thick slices of whole wheat bread for this yam, tomato, and Provolone cheese filler. Sprinkle on some sprouts and get ready for a super sandwich.

2 tablespoons "light" mayonnaise
4 slices whole wheat bread
1 large yam or sweet potato, cooked and sliced (page 257–258)
1 large tomato, sliced
2 ounces Provolone cheese, sliced
Alfalfa sprouts to taste

Spread 1 tablespoon of the mayonnaise on 2 slices of bread. Top each with half of the yam, tomato, and cheese; finish with alfalfa sprouts to taste. Spread the remaining mayonnaise on the other 2 slices of bread; close the sandwiches.

Wrap each sandwich in a paper towel and place on a large microwavable plate. One at a time, microwave on HIGH for 2 to 4 minutes, or until heated through, rotating once.

Makes 2 sandwiches

SPINACH MELT

This knife-and-fork sandwich is a quick meal when you round it out with salad, fresh fruit, and iced tea. Make it a vitamin C fruit like strawberries or oranges to enhance the iron in the spinach. I sometimes use whole wheat English muffins for the bread.

• •

1 pound fresh spinach, stemmed and rinsed, or 1 package (10 ounces) frozen
    chopped spinach, thawed and squeezed dry
2 tablespoons olive oil
1 medium onion, thinly sliced
½ teaspoon salt
¼ teaspoon freshly ground white pepper
⅛ teaspoon ground nutmeg
4 slices whole wheat bread
4 ounces Swiss cheese, shredded or sliced

• •

If using fresh spinach, place it in a 3-quart casserole without drying it. Cover tightly with a lid or vented plastic wrap and microwave on HIGH for 2 minutes. Drain immediately, cool, squeeze dry, and coarsely chop.

In a 2-quart glass baking dish, combine the olive oil and onion. Microwave on HIGH for 4 to 6 minutes, or until the onion is very tender, stirring once or twice. Add the spinach, salt, pepper, and nutmeg. Stir thoroughly to coat with oil and to

(continued)

(continued)

break up the mixture a bit. Microwave on HIGH for 2 to 4 minutes, or until the spinach is tender and the mixture is heated through.

Place a paper towel on a 12-inch round glass plate or in a 13 × 9-inch baking dish; lay the bread on top. Divide the spinach mixture among the 4 slices of bread. Top with cheese. Microwave on HIGH for 2 to 3 minutes, or until the cheese is melted, rotating the plate once.

Makes 4 servings

GARLIC BREAD

Whole wheat Italian bread is never so good as when it's heated with garlic, cheese, and herbs. I like to use herbes de Provence from the crock (sold in gourmet stores and many supermarkets), but you can substitute any of your favorite fresh or dried ones.

••

5 tablespoons butter, softened
3 tablespoons grated Parmesan cheese
2 to 3 garlic cloves, minced
½ teaspoon herbes de Provence, crumbled
1 medium loaf whole wheat Italian bread (12 ounces)

••

In a small bowl, combine the butter, Parmesan cheese, garlic, and herbs, blending well.

Split the bread in half lengthwise without slicing all the way through. Spread a thin layer of the butter mixture on each side. Close the bread and cut in into slices on a diagonal without cutting all the way through.

Wrap the loaf loosely in paper towels. (If you have a small oven, make 2 packages.) Place the bread on the floor of the oven. Microwave on MEDIUM-HIGH for 2 to 3 minutes (longer if there are 2 packages), or until heated through.

Makes 4 servings

••

HOT CHEESY FRENCH ROLLS

This herbed version of melted cheese is a nifty sandwich treat. Tuck in some slices of tomato or fresh pear to make it different.

1 cup shredded Cheddar cheese (4 ounces)
1 cup shredded Swiss cheese (4 ounces)
¼ cup chopped pitted olives
1 scallion, finely sliced
2 tablespoons Dijon mustard
1 tablespoon chopped chives or 1 teaspoon dried chives
¼ teaspoon freshly ground black pepper
6 French rolls, split

In a small mixing bowl, combine the cheeses, olives, scallion, mustard, chives, and pepper. Spoon about ⅓ cup of the mixture on the bottom half of each roll. Replace the tops of the rolls.

Put a paper towel on a 12-inch round microwavable plate; arrange the sandwiches on top in a circle. Microwave on HIGH for 2 minutes, or until heated through.

Makes 6 sandwiches

N O T E : If you are making only 1 or 2 sandwiches at a time, microwave on HIGH for 30 to 45 seconds.

SPICY CORN BREAD

Treat yourself to a ring mold for this recipe. Besides creating an attractive bread, it guarantees even cooking. Whole kernels of corn, sharp Cheddar cheese, and a jalapeño pepper make this bread almost a side dish unto itself.

1 cup plus 2 tablespoons yellow cornmeal
1 cup unbleached white flour
2 teaspoons baking soda
2 teaspoons sugar
2 eggs, lightly beaten
1½ cups yogurt or buttermilk
½ cup vegetable oil
1 cup cooked corn
1 cup grated sharp Cheddar cheese (4 ounces)
1 jalapeño pepper, finely chopped

Lightly grease a 2-quart round microwavable ring pan. Dust with 2 tablespoons cornmeal and set aside.

In a large mixing bowl, combine 1 cup of cornmeal, the flour, baking soda, and sugar. In a small bowl, mix together the egg, yogurt, and vegetable oil; stir in the corn, cheese, and pepper. Pour all at once into the dry ingredients; stir until just blended.

Spread the batter into the prepared pan, smoothing with a rubber spatula or the back of a spoon. Place the pan onto an inverted microwavable cereal bowl. Microwave on MEDIUM for 6 minutes, rotating the pan once during cooking. Microwave on HIGH for 3 to 6 minutes longer, or until a tester inserted in the middle comes out clean, rotating the pan twice during cooking. Let stand on a heat-resistant surface for 5 to 8 minutes, or until the bread begins to pull away from the pan. Place a rack or serving plate over the pan and invert. Serve warm.

Makes 8 to 10 servings

NOTE: To create a ring mold, grease the outside of a 6-ounce glass and place it in the center of a greased round 1½-quart casserole.

SESAME CREAM BISCUITS

Warm biscuits are always a pleasure to serve. These are lightly flavored with Parmesan cheese for extra enjoyment. They don't brown like traditional biscuits, but they're delicious nonetheless.

¾ cup unbleached white flour
¼ cup whole wheat flour
2 tablespoons grated Parmesan cheese
1½ teaspoons baking powder
¼ teaspoon salt
4 tablespoons cold unsalted butter, cut into small chunks
½ cup heavy cream or milk
2 tablespoons Spicy Sesame Seed Topper (page 225) or toasted sesame seeds (optional)

In a medium bowl, combine the white and whole wheat flours, Parmesan cheese, baking powder, and salt. With a pastry blender or two knives, cut in the butter until the mixture resembles coarse crumbs.

Stir in the heavy cream or milk just until a soft dough is formed. Turn out onto a lightly floured surface. Gently knead for about 1 minute. Roll the dough out about ½ inch thick. With a 2½-inch cutter, cut the dough into 8 rounds.

Arrange the biscuits in a circle around the outside of a 12-inch round glass plate. Sprinkle with sesame topping or seeds. Place the plate onto an inverted microwave dish with sides. Microwave on MEDIUM for 5 to 7 minutes, or until the biscuits are puffed, rotating and rearranging twice during cooking. Place on a wire rack and let stand for 3 minutes.

Makes 8 biscuits

ROSEMARY-SCENTED SPOON BREAD

A typical Southern dish, spoon bread is a soft custardlike dish. There are many variations, and I've even had some that were quite firm; you can cook this one to whatever consistency you like. This is a highly nutritious bread considering it contains milk, eggs, and cornmeal; it would be perfect with a salad or steamed vegetable meal. Spoon bread usually takes about 45 minutes to bake in a conventional oven—in the microwave it takes less than 10 minutes.

2½ cups milk
3 tablespoons unsalted butter
1 cup cornmeal
3 eggs
2 teaspoons sugar
1½ teaspoons baking powder
1½ teaspoons chopped rosemary or ¾ teaspoon dried rosemary
¾ teaspoon salt
¼ teaspoon freshly ground white pepper

Place the milk and butter in a 2-quart microwavable casserole or oval dish. Microwave on HIGH for 3 to 4 minutes, or until the milk is heated through and hot but not boiling. Stir in the cornmeal. Microwave, uncovered, on HIGH for 2 to 3 minutes, or until slightly thickened, stirring once.

In a medium bowl, whisk together the eggs, sugar, baking powder, rosemary, salt, and pepper until well combined. Whisk the egg mixture into the cornmeal mixture.

Microwave on MEDIUM for 6 to 8 minutes, or until the center is almost set. Let stand for 5 minutes.

Makes 4 servings

GOOD EARTH SANDWICH

Find some ten-grain bread if you can for this super sandwich. A whole wheat pita pocket is also good for holding it all together.

1 tablespoon Dijon or sharp mustard
2 slices grain bread
2 slices Munster cheese (2 ounces)
½ small avocado (6 ounces), peeled and thinly sliced
2 to 3 thin slices tomato
½ cup alfalfa sprouts, loosely packed

Spread the mustard on both slices of bread. Lay a slice of cheese on 1 piece; top with the avocado, tomato, sprouts, remaining slice of cheese and bread. Wrap the sandwich in 2 unperforated paper towels. Microwave on HIGH for 1½ to 2 minutes, or until the cheese is melted.

Makes 1 sandwich

MINI MUFFIN PIZZAS

If you vary the colors of the peppers and the type of cheese, you can create a different pizza every time. For added convenience, keep some toasted English muffins in the freezer. Add a topping and they're practically ready to serve.

1 small red, green, or yellow bell pepper, seeded and thinly sliced
2 scallions, white parts with about 1 inch of green parts, thinly sliced
2 cups shredded Swiss cheese (8 ounces)
4 English muffins, split and toasted
1 jalapeño pepper, seeded and thinly sliced

(continued)

(continued)

Evenly divide the red, green, or yellow pepper, scallions, and cheese on top of each muffin half; top with the sliced jalapeño.

Place a paper towel on a 12-inch round microwavable glass plate or platter. Arrange 4 or 5 of the pizzas on top. Microwave on MEDIUM for 4 to 5 minutes, or until the cheese is melted, rotating once. Repeat with the remaining pizzas.

Makes 8 pizzas

FIVE-MINUTE MEXICAN PIZZA

Introduce kids to cooking with this fast and nutritious version of pizza. Grown-up tastes might like it served with salsa on the side.

½ cup canned vegetarian refried beans
1 large whole wheat or flour tortilla, 10 inches in diameter
⅔ cup grated Monterey Jack cheese (3 ounces)
2 tablespoons canned chilies, drained

Place beans in a small microwavable dish. Microwave on HIGH for 40 seconds; set aside.

Pierce the tortilla with a fork 2 or 3 times. Brush both sides lightly with water and place between 2 paper towels. Microwave on HIGH for 40 to 60 seconds, or until the tortilla is warmed and almost dry.

Set the tortilla on a round microwavable plate. Spread beans over the center, leaving a ½-inch border; sprinkle with cheese and chilies. Microwave on HIGH for 1 to 1½ minutes, or until the cheese melts.

Makes 1 serving

BREAKFAST AND BRUNCH

Puffy Omelet

Cream Cheese and Chive Omelet

Swiss Chard and Feta Frittata

Ten-Minute Granola

Forty-Carrot Barley Breakfast

Country Breakfast Cereal

Apricot-Orange–Double Oat Cereal

Breakfast Burrito

Fruited Cheese Pocket

Glazed Grapefruit

Harvest Fruit Compote

Cocoa-Applesauce Muffins

Banana–Date Bran Muffins

Raisin–Oat Bran Muffins

Fresh Pear Muffins

Company Cocoa

Single-Serve Cocoa

Morning Zinger

Cranberry-Orange Pleaser

When you own a microwave oven, there's always time for breakfast. Whether it's hot cereal with dried fruits or a mug of hot cocoa, breakfast gets everyone off to a better start.

There's a wide variety here from which to choose. The Ten-Minute Granola can be made ahead and packed in plastic bags; the Breakfast Burrito is the perfect portable meal as is the Fruited Cheese Pocket, which uses a whole wheat pita to hold cream cheese, dried fruit, and coconut. Muffins, a breakfast favorite, are ready in minutes.

PUFFY OMELET

Let this be one of your handiest recipes when you're looking for a quick, no-fuss meal. Add a sweet or savory filling and this omelet is perfect for brunch, lunch, or dinner. I like to spoon some Dried Fruit Chutney (page 219) in the center of my omelet and top it with a dollop of plain yogurt. Some other pleasant filling variations follow the recipe.

2 teaspoons unsalted butter
4 eggs, separated
2 tablespoons milk or water
¼ teaspoon salt
Dash paprika
Fillings and toppings (see below)

Place the butter in a 10-inch glass pie plate. Microwave on HIGH for 45 seconds to 1 minute, or until melted. Rotate the plate to coat the bottom and sides with butter; set aside.

In a medium bowl, beat the egg whites until stiff but not dry. Place the egg yolks, milk, salt, and paprika in another bowl. Using the same beater, beat the yolks until thick and lemon colored. Using a rubber spatula, gently fold the yolks into the egg whites until completely blended.

Pour the egg mixture into the prepared plate; smooth the top to distribute the mixture evenly. Microwave on HIGH for 2½ to 3 minutes, or until just set, rotating the plate once. (Look through the bottom of the plate to see when the omelet is set.) The omelet will puff considerably while cooking, then drop on cooling. Spoon a filling in the center, if desired, then gently fold the omelet in half and slide onto a serving plate.

Makes 2 servings

Fillings and toppings: Caponata (pages 40–41); Vegetarian Chili (pages 105–106); Shredded mozzarella, Swiss, Gouda, or Monterey Jack cheese; Fruit jams or preserves; Mustard Sauce (page 210); Tomato Sauce with Fennel and Mint (page 202); Fresh herbs

CREAM CHEESE AND CHIVE OMELET

For those who prefer a flatter omelet and don't want to be separating and beating the eggs, here's an alternative. The chives are combined with the eggs and the cream cheese is placed in the center at the end. Eggs, cream cheese, and chives are a wonderful trio; try this.

2 teaspoons unsalted butter
4 eggs
¼ cup milk or water
2 tablespoons chopped chives or 1 tablespoon dried chives
Pinch salt
2 tablespoons cream cheese, softened and cut into 1-inch cubes
Freshly ground black pepper

Place the butter in a 9-inch glass pie plate. Microwave on HIGH for 1 minute, or until melted. Rotate the plate to coat with butter; set aside.

In a medium bowl, whisk together the eggs, milk, chives, and salt. Pour into the prepared plate. Microwave on HIGH for 2½ to 4½ minutes, gently pushing the eggs from the edges to the center several times, until the eggs are just set but still moist and creamy.

Place the cheese over the top. Gently fold the omelet in half. Sprinkle with pepper and serve.

Makes 2 servings

SWISS CHARD AND FETA FRITTATA

Swiss chard is an excellent source of vitamin A, potassium, iron, and some calcium—we often forget how rich in nutrients it is. Blend it with feta cheese and eggs; the result is a main dish that is delicious as well as nutritious.

2 tablespoons olive oil
2 garlic cloves, minced
2 cups shredded Swiss chard
6 eggs
⅓ cup milk
4 ounces feta cheese, crumbled
¼ cup canned roasted red peppers, drained and coarsely chopped
2 tablespoons chopped basil or 1 tablespoon dried basil
⅛ teaspoon freshly ground white pepper

In a 9-inch glass pie plate or quiche dish, combine the oil and garlic. Microwave on HIGH for 2 minutes. Add the Swiss chard, stirring to coat with oil. Cover loosely with plastic wrap. Microwave on HIGH for 2 minutes, or until the chard is wilted and tender. Stir and set aside.

In a medium bowl, whisk the eggs and milk together until well blended. Stir in the feta, red peppers, basil, and pepper.

Pour the egg mixture over the chard and stir lightly to combine. Microwave on MEDIUM for 12 to 16 minutes, or until almost set in the center, rotating the dish once. Let stand on a heat-resistant surface for 3 minutes.

Cut into wedges and serve immediately.

Makes 4 servings

TEN-MINUTE GRANOLA

This quick-to-fix cereal is ready in a snap. It stores well so consider doing several batches at a time. Oats, seeds, and nuts give it a high fiber profile with lots of B vitamins.

1½ cups rolled oats
⅓ cup wheat germ
¼ cup sunflower seeds
¼ cup coarsely chopped pecans or walnuts
¼ cup sesame seeds
¼ cup shredded coconut
3 tablespoons packed brown sugar
1 teaspoon ground cinnamon
¼ cup honey
3 tablespoons vegetable oil
½ cup raisins

In an 11 × 7-inch microwavable baking dish, combine the oats, wheat germ, sunflower seeds, nuts, sesame seeds, coconut, brown sugar, and cinnamon. Drizzle honey and oil over the mixture. Stir thoroughly to coat. Gently spread with a spatula or the back of a spoon to make an even layer. Microwave on HIGH for 2 minutes. Stir, making sure to reach the corners of the dish. Gently smooth the layer again. Microwave on HIGH for 3 to 5 minutes, or until the oatmeal is slightly crisp. Stir in the raisins. Let the mixture cool in the dish, stirring occasionally. As it cools, the granola will become crisp and chunky, depending on how much it is stirred. Store in an airtight container.

Makes about 4 cups

FORTY-CARROT BARLEY BREAKFAST

Flecks of carrot add color and vitamin A to this yummy breakfast cereal. A perfect choice for any meal, barley is low in fat and high in soluble fiber; it is also cholesterol- and sodium-free. Vary the fruits in this dish by using peaches or apples instead of pears. I don't usually peel the fruit, but do so if you prefer. Serve maple syrup or brown sugar for a bit of extra sweetness.

3 cups cooked barley (page 259)
¾ cup milk
1 5½-ounce can pear nectar (¾ cup)
2 medium pears, cored and diced (about 8 ounces each)
1 small carrot, finely grated (about 1 cup)
¾ teaspoon ground cinnamon

In a 3-quart microwavable casserole, combine the barley, milk, nectar, pears, carrot, and cinnamon. Cover tightly with a lid or vented plastic wrap. Microwave on HIGH for 4 to 7 minutes, or until slightly thickened, stirring once.

Let stand, covered, for 3 minutes. Stir thoroughly and serve.

Makes 4 servings

NOTE: Cooked barley freezes beautifully in an airtight container or plastic bag for up to 1 month. To reheat 3 cups of frozen barley, microwave on HIGH for 6 to 8 minutes; fluff with a fork.

COUNTRY BREAKFAST CEREAL

Fragrant with cinnamon and sweetened with raisins or dates, this brown-rice breakfast puts warmth into any day. If you like, replace some of the water with milk for extra protein and calcium. Either way, serve the cereal with milk, honey, or brown sugar, and fresh fruit.

1 cup brown rice
2¼ cups water
1 tablespoon butter or margarine
½ cup chopped dates or raisins
1 teaspoon ground cinnamon

Combine all the ingredients in a 3-quart microwavable casserole. Cover tightly with a lid or vented plastic wrap. Microwave on HIGH for 4 to 6 minutes, or until boiling. Reduce setting to MEDIUM and microwave for 30 minutes, or until the water is absorbed. Stir with a fork and serve.

Makes 4 to 6 servings

APRICOT-ORANGE–DOUBLE OAT CEREAL

Oatmeal and oat bran combine with orange juice and dried apricots for a powerhouse breakfast. Serve it with your favorite topping—warm milk, maple syrup, or brown sugar. Personally, I think it's great as is.

2 cups orange juice
2 cups water
1 cup old-fashioned oatmeal
⅔ cup oat bran

½ cup chopped dried apricots
½ teaspoon ground cinnamon

In a 3-quart microwavable casserole, combine all the ingredients. Microwave on HIGH for 8 to 9 minutes, or until the cereal begins to thicken. Stir well before serving to prevent lumping. Let stand, covered, for 3 minutes.

Makes 4 servings

BREAKFAST BURRITO

This warmed-up cream cheese and jelly packet is a perfect breakfast sandwich. Use your favorite jam or any of the homemade fruit spreads from Easy Enhancements (pages 215–229).

2 tablespoons cream cheese
1 large whole wheat tortilla, 10 inches in diameter
1 tablespoon fruit jelly or jam

Spread cream cheese along the middle of the tortilla in about a 2-inch strip. Spoon jam on top of the cheese. Fold the bottom flap over the cheese, fold in the sides, and roll the tortilla to make a snug packet.

Wrap the tortilla loosely in a paper towel. Microwave on MEDIUM for 1 to 1½ minutes. Let stand, wrapped, for 1 minute.

Makes 1 serving

NOTE: Neufchâtel cheese is an excellent substitute for cream cheese. It has 25 percent less fat and 20 percent fewer calories.

FRUITED CHEESE POCKET

This breakfast pita pocket can be prepared the night before, then simply heated in the morning.

1 3-ounce package cream cheese
⅓ cup chopped dried fruit, such as raisins, dates, apricots, etc.
2 tablespoons chopped walnuts
2 tablespoons shredded coconut
⅛ teaspoon ground cinnamon
1 6-inch whole wheat pita bread, cut in half
Honey (optional)

Unwrap the cream cheese and place on a small microwavable plate. Microwave on MEDIUM for 30 seconds, or until the cheese is soft. Stir in dried fruit, walnuts, coconut, and cinnamon, blending well.

Fill each pita half with half of the cheese mixture. Place the pockets, cut side out, on a paper plate. Cover loosely with plastic wrap or a paper towel. Microwave on HIGH for 1 minute, or until heated through. Drizzle with honey, if desired.

Makes 2 servings

GLAZED GRAPEFRUIT

Here's a nifty way to get a quick fix of vitamin C in minutes. Even the most sour grapefruit is tamed with a bit of brown sugar and cinnamon. Grapefruit should be smooth, thin skinned and flat at both ends. For extra eye appeal, choose a Ruby Red or Foster Pink.

2 medium grapefruits
3 tablespoons packed brown sugar
1 teaspoon ground cinnamon
¼ teaspoon ground ginger
Pinch ground nutmeg
1 tablespoon butter or margarine, cut in cubes
4 teaspoons orange juice (optional)
Mint leaves, for garnish

Cut grapefruits in half and remove the seeds with the tip of a sharp knife. Cut around each section to loosen the flesh.

In a small bowl, combine the brown sugar, cinnamon, ginger, and nutmeg. Place the grapefruit halves on a 12-inch microwavable glass plate. Dot with butter. Sprinkle the brown-sugar mixture over each half. Pour 1 teaspoon orange juice over the top of each, if desired. Microwave on HIGH for 6 to 8 minutes, or until warm, rotating the plate once. Garnish with mint leaves.

Makes 4 servings

NOTE: For 2 halves, microwave for 3 to 4 minutes; for 1 half, microwave for 2 minutes.

HARVEST FRUIT COMPOTE

This not-just-for-breakfast compote combines dried and fresh fruits. Vary the fruits with the seasons, perhaps trying fresh peaches and peach nectar in summer instead of apples and apple juice. Don't be afraid to double the recipe: This compote stores well in the refrigerator and is always a welcome treat.

1 package (8 ounces) dried mixed fruit
1 cup unsweetened apple juice
1 teaspoon almond extract
1 teaspoon ground cinnamon
2 medium apples, cored and cut into ½-inch pieces
¼ cup water
2 tablespoons flaked coconut, toasted (see Note)

Sort out the prunes from the dried fruit and remove the pits; cut the larger fruits in half.

In a 2-quart microwavable casserole, combine the dried fruit, including the prunes, apple juice, almond extract, and cinnamon. Cover tightly with a lid or vented plastic wrap. Microwave on HIGH for 5 minutes, or until heated through.

Stir in the apples and water. Re-cover and microwave on HIGH for 5 minutes. Let stand, covered, for 5 minutes.

Divide the fruit mixture evenly into four small dishes. Garnish with toasted coconut.

Makes 4 servings

N O T E : To toast coconut, place 2 tablespoons flaked coconut in a 1-cup glass measure. Microwave on HIGH for 1 to 2 minutes, or until light brown, stirring every 30 seconds.

COCOA-APPLESAUCE MUFFINS

Cocoa is a good way to enjoy the full taste of chocolate while limiting saturated fat. I have used olive oil here with excellent results, but any mild vegetable oil will do the trick.

Cocoa Crunch Topping (page 226)
¼ cup Hershey's cocoa
¼ cup vegetable oil
¾ cup unsweetened applesauce
1 egg, beaten
½ cup chopped nuts
¾ cup unbleached white flour
½ cup whole wheat flour
⅓ cup sugar
¾ teaspoon baking soda
½ teaspoon ground cinnamon
¼ teaspoon salt (optional)

Prepare the topping and set aside. Place a double layer of paper baking cups in a microwavable cupcake or muffin pan.

In a small bowl, combine the cocoa and oil; stir until smooth. Add the applesauce, egg, and nuts; blend well.

In a medium bowl, combine the white and whole wheat flours, sugar, baking soda, cinnamon, and salt, if using. Add the applesauce mixture, stirring just until the dry ingredients are moistened.

Fill muffin cups half full with half the batter. Sprinkle a heaping teaspoonful of topping on top of each muffin. Microwave on HIGH for 2 to 3½ minutes, or until a wooden pick inserted in the center comes out clean, turning a half turn after each minute. (Tops may still appear moist, but spots will disappear upon standing.) Remove muffins from the cups to a wire rack immediately. If any moisture has formed in the muffin cups, wipe with a paper towel. Repeat procedure with the remaining batter. Serve warm.

Makes 12 muffins

N O T E : For low-cholesterol baking, 2 egg whites can be substituted for 1 whole egg.

BANANA–DATE BRAN MUFFINS

The batter for these muffins keeps in the refrigerator for up to a month, so don't worry that this recipe yields about 30 muffins. The fat content is exceptionally low, so you wind up with a muffin just under 150 calories! With prepared mix in the fridge and microwave time under 5 minutes, is there any reason not to have fresh muffins every day?

3 eggs
2⅓ cups yogurt or buttermilk
1 cup orange juice
⅓ cup honey or molasses
⅓ cup packed brown sugar
¼ cup vegetable oil
1 medium-size ripe banana, cut in thirds
1 tablespoon ground cinnamon
2 teaspoons vanilla
1 teaspoon ground cardamom
3 cups bran cereal
½ cup chopped dates
1½ cups unbleached white flour
1 cup whole wheat flour
1 tablespoon baking soda
½ teaspoon salt (optional)

Place a double layer of paper baking cups in a microwavable cupcake or muffin pan.

Blend the eggs, yogurt, orange juice, honey, brown sugar, oil, banana, cinnamon, vanilla, and cardamom in a food processor or blender until combined but banana is still a bit chunky.

Place the cereal in a large mixing bowl and stir in the egg mixture and dates until thoroughly combined. Let stand in 15 minutes.

Sift the white and whole wheat flour, baking soda, and salt, if using, over the bran mixture. Stir until just combined. Fill muffin cups three-fourths full with some of the batter. Microwave on HIGH for 3 to 4 minutes, or until a wooden pick inserted in the center comes out clean. Rotate once during cooking. (Tops may still appear moist, but spots will disappear on standing.)

Remove muffins from the cups to a wire rack immediately. If any moisture has formed in the muffin cups, wipe with a paper towel. Repeat procedure for as many muffins as desired. Cover and refrigerate remaining batter for up to 1 month.

Makes about 30 muffins

N O T E : All of the batter can be prepared ahead and then used whenever you like. Be sure to cover tightly and keep refrigerated.

RAISIN—OAT BRAN MUFFINS

Oat bran was the first of the soluble fibers to be touted for its cholesterol-lowering benefits. We now know that rice bran, legumes, and fruits may be as good or better. In any event, these muffins are still a pleasant way to start the day.

2 cups oat bran
1 teaspoon baking powder
1 teaspoon baking soda
1 teaspoon ground cinnamon
½ teaspoon ground nutmeg
1 cup yogurt or buttermilk
¼ cup molasses
1 egg or 2 egg whites
¼ cup vegetable oil
2 tablespoons packed brown sugar
1 teaspoon vanilla
½ cup raisins

(continued)

(continued)

Place a double layer of paper baking cups in a microwavable cupcake or muffin pan.

In a large bowl, combine the oat bran, baking powder, baking soda, cinnamon, and nutmeg.

In a medium bowl, combine the yogurt, molasses, egg, oil, brown sugar, and vanilla. Make a well in the center of the dry ingredients and add the yogurt mixture. Stir just to combine. Fold in raisins.

Fill muffin cups three-fourths full with half the batter. Microwave on HIGH for 3 to 4 minutes, or until a wooden pick inserted in the center comes out clean. Rotate once during cooking. Be careful not to overcook. (Tops may still appear moist, but spots will disappear on standing.)

Remove muffins from the cups to a wire rack immediately. If any moisture has formed in the cups, wipe with a paper towel. Repeat cooking procedure with remaining batter.

Makes 12 muffins

NOTE: Freeze muffins if desired and reheat on HIGH for 30 to 45 seconds for each muffin.

FRESH PEAR MUFFINS

Muffins made of rice bran, sunflower seeds, and fresh pears are a quick and flavorful way to start the day. Because rice bran is so fine, I whisk it with the flour and baking powder for a better blend. I'll often use a plain or flavored Edensoy milk if any of my guests are avoiding whole milk.

1¼ cups whole wheat flour
1 cup rice bran
¼ cup sunflower seeds
2 teaspoons baking powder
¼ teaspoon salt
1 egg

··

1 cup milk
⅓ cup vegetable oil
½ cup packed brown sugar
1 medium pear (about 6 ounces), peeled, cored, and diced

··

Place a double layer of paper baking cups in a microwavable cupcake or muffin pan.

In a large bowl, combine the flour, rice bran, sunflower seeds, baking powder, and salt with a wire whisk to distribute the ingredients evenly.

In a medium bowl, whisk together the egg, milk, vegetable oil, and brown sugar. Stir in the chopped pear.

Make a well in the center of the flour mixture; pour in the egg mixture. Stir until just combined.

Fill muffin cups three-fourths full with half the batter. Microwave on HIGH for 2 to 2½ minutes, or until a wooden pick inserted in the center comes out clean. Rotate once during cooking. (Tops may still appear moist, but spots will disappear on standing.)

Remove muffins to a wire rack immediately. If any moisture has formed in the muffin cups, wipe with a paper towel. Repeat with the remaining batter. Serve warm.

Makes 12 muffins

N O T E : If your muffins are not done after 2 minutes, continue cooking in 10-second intervals to prevent dry, overcooked muffins. I found 2 minutes was perfect in the 650-watt oven I used for testing these muffins.

N O T E : Be sure that your rice bran stays fresh. Store it in an airtight container, in the refrigerator, for up to 6 months. Otherwise it will deteriorate and taste bitter.

··

COMPANY COCOA

Take an extra minute to add grated orange peel and vanilla to this hot chocolate. It's a great afternoon pick-me-up and a nice change from after-dinner coffee, especially for those trying to cut down on caffeine.

¼ cup unsweetened cocoa
¼ cup sugar
3 cups milk
2 teaspoons grated orange peel, orange part only
1 teaspoon vanilla
Ground cinnamon, for garnish

In a 4-cup glass measure, combine the cocoa, sugar, and about ¼ cup of the milk; stir until smooth. Stir in the remaining milk, orange peel, and vanilla. Microwave on HIGH for 5 to 7 minutes, or until hot. Stir to blend. Pour into mugs or cups. Sprinkle with cinnamon and serve.

Makes 4 servings

SINGLE-SERVE COCOA

We really don't ever outgrow our need for milk, though many adults drink little or none of it. Here's a quick way to get a head start on your protein and calcium for the day. If you are "non-dairy," try vanilla Edensoy for a nicely flavored blend, made with natural soy milk.

2 teaspoons sugar
1 heaping teaspoon unsweetened cocoa
1 cup milk

In a microwavable cup or mug, combine the sugar, cocoa, and about 1 tablespoon of the milk; stir until smooth. Stir in remaining milk. Microwave on HIGH for 1½ minutes, or until hot. Stir to blend.

Makes 1 serving

MORNING ZINGER

Here's a way of winding down from caffeine that is quick to fix anytime of day, not just in the morning. Check your tea bags carefully as some have staples, which will cause arcing or sparks in the oven. (Celestial Seasonings herb teas do not.)

. . . .

6 Zinger (red, orange, or lemon) herb tea bags
3 cups water
¼ cup honey
4 cinnamon sticks (3 inches each)
4 cloves

. . . .

Place the tea bags in a 4-cup glass measure; add water. Microwave on HIGH for 3 to 4 minutes, or until boiling. Let stand for 3 minutes.

Remove the tea bags; stir in the honey, cinnamon sticks, and cloves. Microwave on MEDIUM for 6 minutes. Strain into mugs. Garnish with the cinnamon sticks, if desired.

Makes 4 servings

CRANBERRY-ORANGE PLEASER

This cheery juice combo is a refreshing change from orange juice, especially on chilly mornings. It's also nice in the afternoon, much better than carbonated soft drinks.

1⅓ cups cranberry juice cocktail
⅔ cup fresh orange juice
1 cinnamon stick, 2 to 3 inches long
Orange slices, for garnish (optional)

In a 4-cup glass measure, combine the cranberry juice, orange juice, and cinnamon stick. Microwave on HIGH for 3 to 4 minutes, or until the juice is just boiling. Pour into mugs. Garnish with orange slices, if desired.

Makes 2 servings

MAIN ATTRACTIONS

No-Sweat Lasagne
Lasagne Florentine Rolls
Whole Wheat Vegetable Lasagne
Linguine with Fresh Vegetables and Herbs
Spaghetti with Japanese Eggplant
Baked Macaroni with Carrots and Broccoli
Baked Macaroni and Cheese
Red Beans and Rice
Spicy Black Beans
Carol's Calico Chili
Vegetarian Chili
Indian Dal
Lentil Stew
Couscous and Spicy Vegetable Stew
Polenta
Southern Grits Casserole
Risotto with Asparagus, Mushrooms, and Fontina
Risotto with Peas
Risotto with Beans
Tempeh and Napa Stir-Fry
Vietnamese Pho
Thai Vegetable Curry
Tofu and Cellophane Noodle Salad
Asian Noodle Salad
Sushi

(continued)

(continued)

Vegetarian Paella
Job's Multigrain Casserole
Ratatouille
Vegetable Kabobs
Cauliflower Stew
Stuffed Acorn Squash
Stuffed Chayote
Stuffed Peppers
Three-Bread Stuffing
Main Meal-stuffed Potatoes
Oriental stuffed Potatoes
Stuffed Eggplant
Zucchini-Corn Strata
Cheese Enchiladas

Ethnic recipes are what make vegetarian menus so exciting. The wide variety of herbs and the new flavors used help to break the cycle of familiar meals. Vegetarian food has the unfortunate—and sometimes deserved, I'm afraid—reputation of being dull, bland, and unsatisfying. I hope that notion will change once you have tried these dishes.

Here you will find a wide assortment of recipes from which to choose. Italian, Thai, Vietnamese, and Mexican, along with some American favorites, will provide lots of opportunities to prove that meals need never be boring again.

Whether you are a vegetarian, would like to be, or just want to find out if it is possible to really "cook" in the microwave, a new dimension in pleasurable eating is waiting for you. For the cholesterol-conscious, many of the dishes contain little fat and cholesterol. Be assured that there are lots of easy, pleasing recipes for everyone to enjoy.

NO-SWEAT LASAGNE

The worst part of making lasagne is cooking the noodles. Large steamy pots of boiling water are unwieldy, and testing the noodles can be a bit tricky. Using uncooked noodles, this recipe assembles and cooks faster than any you've ever tried. If you're cooking for a crowd or want to freeze an extra batch, just double the ingredients, use two 11 × 7-inch dishes, and cook them one at a time.

1 15-ounce container ricotta cheese (2 cups)
2 eggs, lightly beaten
½ cup grated Parmesan cheese, divided
¼ cup chopped parsley
¾ teaspoon salt
¼ teaspoon freshly ground black pepper
9 lasagne noodles, uncooked
4 cups Chunky Tomato Sauce (page 203)
2 cups grated mozzarella cheese (8 ounces)

In a large bowl, combine the ricotta cheese, eggs, half of the Parmesan cheese, parsley, salt, and pepper. Mix well until thoroughly blended.

Pour 1 cup of sauce into an 11 × 7-inch microwavable baking dish. Spread the sauce evenly to cover the bottom of the dish. Arrange 3 noodles in a single layer on top of the sauce. Spoon one-third of the ricotta cheese mixture over the noodles. Sprinkle with about one-third each of the remaining Parmesan and the mozzarella. Pour 1 cup sauce over the cheese. Arrange another layer of noodles, cheese, and sauce on top. Repeat, using the remaining ingredients. Cover tightly with vented plastic wrap. Microwave on MEDIUM for 12 to 18 minutes, or until the noodles are just tender when pierced with the tip of a sharp knife and the sauce is bubbling. Rotate twice during cooking. Let stand, covered, for 15 minutes.

Makes 6 servings

LASAGNE FLORENTINE ROLLS

These colorful spinach and cheese lasagne rolls are as delicious as they are attractive. At Christmas, when I serve a variety of hot and cold appetizers and desserts rather than a traditional dinner, I like to color-coordinate the foods so that most of them are red, white, and green. When these rolls are cut in half and placed upright on a platter of tomato sauce, the visual impact is quite impressive. Since we are talking about main courses here, allow two rolls per person for a satisfying entree.

1 whole egg
1 egg yolk
2 10-ounce packages frozen spinach, thawed and well drained
1 cup ricotta cheese
1 cup grated mozzarella cheese
½ cup grated Romano cheese
2 garlic cloves, minced
2 tablespoons chopped parsley
½ teaspoon freshly ground black pepper
¼ teaspoon salt
¼ teaspoon ground nutmeg
8 lasagne noodles, cooked al dente (12–15 minutes) in rapidly boiling water with
   1 tablespoon oil added to the water
2 cups Tomato Sauce with Fennel and Mint (page 202)

In a large bowl, beat the egg and egg yolk together. Squeeze any excess water out of the spinach and add it, the ricotta, mozzarella, Romano, garlic, parsley, pepper, salt, and nutmeg to the eggs. Mix together until thoroughly combined.

Using a large sheet of wax paper, lay out the lasagne noodles, one at a time. Use a paper towel to wipe off any excess moisture. Spread about ¼ cup of the spinach mixture along the entire length of each noodle, using the back of the spoon to distribute evenly. Leave about ½ inch uncovered at each end. Roll up the noodles to enclose the filling.

Pour 1 cup of sauce onto a 12-inch microwavable round glass plate and spread it out so that it covers the plate, leaving a 1-inch border. Arrange the rolls on the plate, seam side down, in a circle. Cover tightly with vented plastic wrap.

Microwave on MEDIUM for 10 to 14 minutes, or until the center part of each roll is heated through and the cheese is melted. Let stand, covered, for 5 minutes.

While the lasagne rolls are standing, pour the remaining sauce into a 2-cup glass measure. Microwave on HIGH for 2 minutes to heat through. Remove the cover from the lasagne rolls, pour sauce over the top, and serve.

Makes 8 rolls

WHOLE WHEAT VEGETABLE LASAGNE

Fresh vegetables and a touch of crushed red pepper really pick up the taste of whole wheat pasta. This can be a nice summer dish since the noodles aren't cooked first and there's no hot pot to watch over. There will be more liquid than usual because of the water given off by the vegetables. Chunky Tomato Sauce (page 203) is very flavorful and makes a nice light sauce to spoon around the lasagne.

1 15-ounce container ricotta cheese (2 cups)
2 eggs, lightly beaten
½ cup grated Parmesan cheese, divided
¼ cup chopped parsley
½ teaspoon salt
¼ teaspoon crushed red pepper
9 whole wheat lasagne noodles, uncooked
3 cups Chunky Tomato Sauce (page 203)
1 cup thinly sliced zucchini
1 cup thinly sliced mushrooms
1 cup grated carrots
¼ cup oil-cured olives, pitted and chopped
2 cups grated mozzarella cheese (8 ounces)

In a large bowl, combine the ricotta cheese, eggs, half of the Parmesan cheese, parsley, salt, and red pepper. Mix well until thoroughly blended.

(continued)

(continued)

Pour 1 cup of the sauce into an 11 × 7-inch microwavable baking dish. Spread sauce evenly to cover the bottom of the dish. Arrange 3 noodles in a single layer on top of the sauce. Spoon one-third of the cheese mixture over the noodles. Arrange about one-third each of the zucchini, mushrooms, carrots, and olives on top. Sprinkle with about one-third each of the remaining Parmesan and the mozzarella. Pour about ¾ cup of sauce over the cheeses. Arrange another layer of noodles, cheese, and vegetables on top. Repeat, using the remaining ingredients. Cover tightly with vented plastic wrap. Microwave on MEDIUM for 12 to 18 minutes, or until the noodles are just tender and the sauce is bubbling. Rotate twice during cooking. (The noodles should be al dente but not crisp. They will continue to cook on standing and be fine when ready to serve.) Let stand, covered, for 15 minutes.

Makes 6 servings

LINGUINE WITH FRESH VEGETABLES AND HERBS

It's a sure sign summer has arrived when you prepare this entree. Tossing the pasta with olive oil and mustard gives it a light coating rather than a saucy personality. Asparagus, yellow squash, and chives also heightens the flavor. As with most pasta dishes, I pass some crushed red pepper for guests who like theirs spicier.

5 tablespoons olive oil
2 shallots, minced
4 tablespoons Dijon mustard
1 pound asparagus, trimmed and cut on the diagonal into 1-inch pieces
2 tablespoons water
1 medium yellow squash, diced (about 6 ounces)
½ cup shelled peas or frozen peas, defrosted
¼ cup chopped Italian parsley
3 tablespoons chopped chives or 1 tablespoon dried chives
¾ teaspoon freshly ground black pepper

• •

1 pound thin linguine, cooked
Salt to taste

• •

Place oil and shallots in a 1-cup glass measure. Microwave on HIGH for 2 minutes. Stir in mustard and set aside.

Place asparagus in a 2-quart microwavable casserole and sprinkle with 2 tablespoons water. Cover tightly with vented plastic wrap. Microwave on HIGH for 2 minutes. Add squash and fresh peas (hold frozen peas to toss in at final stage) and stir to combine. Re-cover and microwave on HIGH for 4 minutes. Let stand, covered, for 2 minutes.

In a large serving bowl, toss cooked linguine with the dressing, vegetables (including frozen peas, if using), parsley, chives, and pepper. Season with salt to taste and additional pepper, if desired.

Makes 4 servings

SPAGHETTI WITH JAPANESE EGGPLANT

Small Japanese eggplant tend to be less bitter than their larger cousins. You can also serve this sauce over Chinese or Japanese noodles and sprinkle the dish with some toasted sesame seeds for extra crunch.

• •

¼ cup olive oil
2 garlic cloves, minced
1 small onion, finely chopped
½ medium fennel bulb, trimmed and chopped
½ medium red bell pepper, cut into julienne strips
½ medium yellow bell pepper, cut into julienne strips
3 Japanese eggplants (about 12 ounces), diced
1 16-ounce can whole tomatoes, drained (juices reserved) and finely chopped
1 teaspoon dried thyme
½ teaspoon freshly ground black pepper
1 pound thin spaghetti or Japanese noodles, cooked

(continued)

• •

In a 3-quart microwavable casserole, combine oil, garlic, onion, and fennel. Microwave on HIGH for 3 to 4 minutes, or until the onion is tender. Stir in peppers, eggplant, tomatoes and about ½ cup of their juices, thyme, and pepper, tossing well. Cover tightly with a lid or vented plastic wrap. Microwave on HIGH for 8 to 10 minutes, or until the vegetables are tender. Let stand, covered, for 2 minutes. Place the spaghetti in a large serving bowl, spoon sauce over the top, and serve.

Makes 4 servings

BAKED MACARONI WITH CARROTS AND BROCCOLI

This homey favorite is studded with small broccoli florets and chunks of carrot. Like the lasagne, the elbow macaroni is not precooked; nor is it necessary to precook the broccoli and carrots. They all steam together for the easiest version of this comfort food that you'll ever find. Use a Wisconsin Cheddar for extra flavor.

2 tablespoons butter or oil
2 tablespoons unbleached white flour
2 cups milk
1½ cups water
2 cups uncooked elbow macaroni (8 ounces)
1 cup carrot pieces (½ inch)
1 cup small broccoli florets
2 cups grated Cheddar cheese (8 ounces)
½ teaspoon salt
½ teaspoon freshly ground white pepper
Pinch ground red pepper

Place the butter in a 3-quart microwavable casserole. Microwave on HIGH for 1 minute, or until melted (or, if using oil, until it is hot). Whisk in flour until smooth.

Microwave on HIGH for 1 minute. Whisk in milk and water. Microwave on HIGH for 4 to 6 minutes, or until very hot and almost boiling, stirring once.

Add macaroni, carrots, and broccoli, stirring thoroughly to combine. Cover tightly with a lid or vented plastic wrap. Microwave on MEDIUM for 10 minutes. Stir in the cheese, salt, white and red pepper. Re-cover and microwave on MEDIUM-LOW for 5 to 7 minutes, or until the cheese is melted and the macaroni is almost cooked. Stir well. (The mixture will appear quite soupy, but it will thicken on standing.) Re-cover and let stand for 10 to 15 minutes, or until creamy and set.

Makes 4 servings

BAKED MACARONI AND CHEESE

If you cling to the notion that pasta must be boiled on top of the stove or if you have some cooked on hand, here's a more traditional recipe.

2 tablespoons vegetable oil
1 tablespoon unbleached white flour
1½ cups milk
4 cups cooked elbow macaroni
2½ cups shredded Cheddar cheese, divided (10 ounces)
½ teaspoon salt
½ teaspoon freshly ground white pepper
Dash Tabasco sauce

Pour the oil into a 3-quart microwavable casserole and whisk in the flour. Microwave on HIGH for 1 minute, or until foamy. Whisk in the milk. Microwave on HIGH for 4 minutes, stirring once. Stir in the macaroni, 2 cups of the cheese, salt, pepper, and Tabasco. Cover loosely with a lid or vented plastic wrap. Microwave on MEDIUM-HIGH for 5 to 6 minutes (longer if the macaroni was not hot and freshly cooked), stirring after 3 minutes. Sprinkle with the remaining cheese. Re-cover and let stand for 5 minutes.

Makes 4 servings

RED BEANS AND RICE

When it comes to complementary proteins, beans and rice are about the best. This simple and spicy version is the perfect reason to keep both cooked rice and cooked beans close at hand. There is no fat or oil in the recipe. It's a showcase for complex carbohydrates at their best. A tossed salad and whole-grain rolls round out the meal. The chopped red onion, olive oil, and red pepper vinegar are traditional condiments served with this dish in the South. Look for the red pepper vinegar (a spicier version of vinegar) in supermarkets and specialty food stores.

2 cups chopped onions
2 garlic cloves, minced
1 bay leaf
¼ teaspoon ground red pepper
2 medium tomatoes, diced, or 1 14-ounce can tomatoes, drained and chopped
1 tablespoon Worcestershire sauce
½ teaspoon Tabasco sauce, or to taste
3 cups cooked red kidney beans (page 251) or canned, drained
Water, if needed
Salt to taste
3 cups hot cooked rice (page 260)
3 tablespoons chopped cilantro
Chopped red onion (optional)
Olive oil (optional)
Red pepper vinegar (optional)

In a 5-quart microwavable casserole, combine the onions, garlic, bay leaf, red pepper, tomatoes, Worcestershire, and Tabasco sauce. Cover tightly with a lid or vented plastic wrap. Microwave on HIGH for 4 to 6 minutes. Stir and rotate once during cooking. Stir in the beans. Re-cover and microwave on MEDIUM for 18 to 24 minutes, stirring after 10 minutes, or until the beans are soft and the mixture has thickened. Add more water if necessary. Let stand, covered, for 5 minutes. Remove bay leaf.

Serve the beans on a bed of rice. Garnish with chopped cilantro. A small bowl of chopped onion and cruets of olive oil and red pepper vinegar may be passed separately to be added to taste, if desired. Otherwise you may want to increase the Worcestershire and Tabasco for a spicier dish.

Makes 6 servings

SPICY BLACK BEANS

Author and food editor Susan Kessler gives flair to black beans by adding goat cheese to this Mexican dish. Serve it on a flour tortilla garnished with shredded lettuce and scallions. The beans are also great as a dip served with chips.

2 cups presoaked black beans (see Note)
3 cups water
5 garlic cloves, peeled, 3 left whole and 2 minced
1 bay leaf
2 jalapeño peppers, seeded and minced
¾ teaspoon ground cumin
12 ounces goat cheese, crumbled
6 medium scallions, thinly sliced
Salt to taste

In a 3-quart microwavable casserole, combine the presoaked beans, water, whole garlic cloves, and bay leaf. Cover tightly and microwave on HIGH for 10 to 15 minutes, or until boiling. Stir, re-cover, and microwave on MEDIUM for 20 to 30 minutes, or until the beans are tender. Drain the beans, reserving the liquid, and transfer to a mixing bowl. Mash the beans, adding enough reserved liquid to make a loose paste. Add the peppers, cumin, half the goat cheese, the scallions, minced garlic, and salt to taste; stir to combine.

Place in a greased gratin dish, top with the remaining cheese, and microwave, uncovered, on MEDIUM for 2 to 3 minutes, or until the cheese melts.

Makes 4 servings

N O T E : To presoak, place 2 cups (about 1 pound) of rinsed and sorted dry beans in a 3-quart microwavable casserole with 3 cups of water. Cover tightly with a lid or vented plastic wrap. Microwave on HIGH for 7 to 12 minutes, or until boiling. Stir, re-cover, and microwave on MEDIUM for 2 minutes. Let stand, covered, for 1 hour. Drain.

CAROL'S CALICO CHILI

This simple and savory chili was developed by Carol Gelles, grain maven and author of *The Complete Whole Grain Cookbook*. The combination of bulgur and beans in this lightly flavored dish makes a complete protein entree. Use canned stewed tomatoes for an even tastier version. Serve it garnished with chopped onions or scallions, if desired.

1 cup chopped onion
¾ cup chopped red bell pepper
¾ cup chopped yellow bell pepper
2 garlic cloves, minced
2 tablespoons vegetable oil
1 tablespoon chili powder
1 teaspoon ground cumin
2 cups Basic Vegetable Stock (page 199)
1 14½-ounce can whole peeled or stewed tomatoes, with juices
1 cup bulgur
2 cups cooked red kidney beans (page 251) or canned (one 16-ounce can), drained
¼ cup chopped parsley
Salt to taste

In a 3-quart microwavable bowl, stir together the onion, red and yellow peppers, and garlic. Stir in the oil. Microwave on HIGH for 3 minutes. Stir in chili powder and cumin until absorbed.

Stir in the stock and tomatoes, breaking up the tomatoes with the back of a spoon. Cover with wax paper and microwave on HIGH for 6 minutes. Stir in the bulgur. Re-cover and microwave on MEDIUM for 15 minutes.

Stir in the beans and parsley. Re-cover and microwave on MEDIUM for 10 minutes. Let stand for 4 minutes. Add salt to taste.

Makes 4 servings

N O T E : The chili will thicken considerably on standing or if it is prepared in advance. Add additional stock or tomato juice to get desired consistency when reheating.

VEGETARIAN CHILI

"This is the 'meatiest' meatless chili I've ever eaten," my friends have been heard to exclaim. The flavors are hearty and full rather than hot and fiery. I like to vary the beans, using two or three different kinds. Look for the best tomatoes you can find or use canned tomatoes. The pale, dull ones detract from a fine finish.

¼ cup olive oil
5 large garlic cloves, minced
1 large onion, coarsely chopped
1 medium red bell pepper, coarsely chopped
1 medium green bell pepper, coarsely chopped
3 tablespoons chili powder
2 tablespoons ground cumin
2 tablespoons chopped oregano or 1 tablespoon dried oregano
2 tablespoons chopped basil or 1 tablespoon dried basil
2 teaspoons anise extract or 1½ teaspoons fennel seeds
2 teaspoons unsweetened cocoa powder
1 teaspoon dried thyme
1 teaspoon ground cinnamon
4 medium tomatoes, coarsely chopped (about 1½ pounds)
2 cups Basic Vegetable Stock (page 199)
6 cups cooked beans, such as kidney or pinto or chick peas or canned,
     (three 15-ounce cans), drained
¼ cup balsamic vinegar
Garnishes (see right)

In a 5-quart microwavable casserole, combine the oil, garlic, onion, red and green peppers and stir well to coat with oil. Cover tightly with a lid or vented plastic wrap. Microwave on HIGH for 3 minutes, or until the vegetables are tender, stirring once during cooking. Stir in the chili powder, cumin, oregano, basil, anise extract, cocoa, thyme, and cinnamon. Microwave, uncovered, on HIGH for 4 minutes, stirring once.

(continued)

(continued)

Stir in tomatoes, stock, and beans. Re-cover and microwave on HIGH for 12 to 15 minutes or until boiling. Uncover, reduce setting to MEDIUM and cook for 15 minutes. Stir in the vinegar. Microwave on MEDIUM for another 30 to 40 minutes, until the flavors are blended and the chili has thickened. Let stand for 10 minutes.

Makes 8 servings

Garnishes: Yogurt or sour cream, chopped cilantro, black olives, chopped scallions, grated Cheddar cheese, and lime wedges

INDIAN DAL

Many Indians enjoy a dal, or lentil dish, at every meal. A good source of protein and an excellent soluble fiber, lentils lend themselves well to a variety of herbs and spices. The ground red pepper make this hotter than many. It's interesting that when it stands for a day or two, the heat disappears and the lemon is accentuated. Serve with Basmati Rice Pilaf (pages 166–167) and steamed spinach.

2 garlic cloves, coarsely chopped
1 cup finely chopped onion
3 tablespoons peanut oil or Clarified Butter (page 208)
2 teaspoons finely chopped ginger
1 teaspoon garam masala (see Note)
1 teaspoon ground turmeric
1 teaspoon ground cumin
½ teaspoon cumin seed
¼ teaspoon ground red pepper
4 curry leaves, see Note (optional)
4 cups water
1½ cups yellow lentils
2 tablespoons chopped coriander (cilantro)
Juice of 1 lemon

• •

In a 3-quart microwavable casserole, combine the garlic, onion, oil, ginger, garam masala, turmeric, ground cumin, cumin seed, red pepper, and curry leaves, if using. Microwave on HIGH for 2 to 3 minutes, or until the onion is tender. Stir in the water and lentils. Cover with a lid or vented plastic wrap. Microwave on HIGH for 12 to 15 minutes, or until boiling. Stir and re-cover. Microwave on MEDIUM for 35 to 40 minutes, or until the lentils are cooked and soft. Stir and rotate twice during the last 15 minutes of cooking. (Add additional water, if necessary.) Stir in coriander and lemon juice. Cover and let stand for 10 minutes.

Makes 6 servings

N O T E : Garam masala and curry leaves are available at Indian and Oriental markets.

N O T E : Dal freezes very well. It's great to keep on hand for a quick dinner. With a quick pilaf or leftover rice, it makes a complete, high-protein meal.

LENTIL STEW

Not nearly as spicy as an Indian dal, this stew is mildly seasoned with just a bay leaf, some thyme, and rosemary. Serve it with a rice pilaf along with a tomato and onion salad.

3 tablespoons peanut oil
3 garlic cloves, minced
1 medium onion, finely chopped
1 celery rib, coarsely chopped
1 medium carrot, peeled and coarsely chopped
1½ cups sliced mushrooms (about 4 ounces)
4½ cups water
1 cup green lentils, rinsed and drained
1 bay leaf
½ teaspoon dried thyme
½ teaspoon dried rosemary
½ teaspoon freshly ground white pepper
1½ tablespoons balsamic vinegar
Salt to taste

In a 3-quart microwavable casserole, combine the oil, garlic, onion, celery, and carrot. Microwave on HIGH for 2 minutes. Stir in the mushrooms and microwave on HIGH for 1 minute. Add the water, lentils, bay leaf, thyme, rosemary, and pepper. Cover tightly with a lid or vented plastic wrap. Microwave on HIGH for 8 to 10 minutes, or until boiling. Stir and partially re-cover. Microwave on MEDIUM for 30 to 40 minutes, or until the lentils are cooked and the stew has thickened slightly, stirring twice.

Remove bay leaf and stir in balsamic vinegar. Re-cover and let stand for 5 to 10 minutes. Add salt to taste.

Makes 4 servings

COUSCOUS AND SPICY VEGETABLE STEW

A semolina-type grain, couscous is the national dish of Morocco. This fragrant and colorful stew is a perfect partner for it.

¼ cup olive oil
2 garlic cloves, minced
1 medium onion, coarsely chopped
½ teaspoon ground coriander
½ teaspoon ground cumin
½ teaspoon ground turmeric
1 medium red bell pepper, cut into 1-inch pieces
1 medium fennel bulb, thinly sliced (about 8 ounces)
2 medium ripe tomatoes, coarsely chopped
1 medium zucchini, cut into ½-inch pieces (about 6 ounces)
½ cup raisins
2 cinnamon sticks (3 inches each)
5 whole cloves
5 black peppercorns, lightly crushed
¼ teaspoon ground red pepper, or to taste
1 cup water
2 cups cooked chick peas or canned (one 15-ounce can), drained
3 cups water
½ teaspoon salt
1½ cups couscous
⅓ cup toasted pine nuts, for garnish (optional)

In a 3-quart microwavable casserole, combine the oil, garlic, onion, coriander, cumin, and turmeric. Microwave on HIGH for 4 to 6 minutes, or until the onion is tender, stirring once. Add the bell pepper and fennel. Microwave on HIGH for 3 minutes.

Stir in the tomatoes, zucchini, raisins, cinnamon, cloves, peppercorns, red pepper and water. Cover tightly with a lid or vented plastic wrap. Microwave on HIGH

(continued)

(continued)

for 5 to 7 minutes, or until boiling. Stir in the chick peas. Re-cover and microwave on MEDIUM for 12 to 15 minutes, or until the vegetables are tender (longer if you prefer them soft). Let stand, covered, for 10 minutes.

Meanwhile, combine the water and salt in a 2-quart microwavable casserole. Microwave on HIGH for 3 to 5 minutes, or until boiling. Stir in couscous. Cover tightly with a lid or vented plastic wrap. Let stand, covered, for 5 to 8 minutes or until the water is absorbed.

When ready to serve, fluff the couscous lightly with a fork, arrange on a large serving platter, and make a hollow in the middle. Ladle stew into the center; remove and discard cinnamon sticks. Garnish with pine nuts, if desired.

Makes 4 to 6 servings

POLENTA

I remember the soft, steamy type of polenta from my childhood. It was served with fresh tomato sauce and sprinkled liberally with grated Parmesan cheese, but other ingredients can also be added, black olives and Gorgonzola cheese to name but two. I've enriched the basic version using some milk instead of all water. Top off the Polenta with one of your favorite tomato sauces or Fresh Mushroom Sauce (page 205). Steamed spinach or fresh asparagus would be a nice side dish here.

1 cup milk
2½ cups water
1 cup stone-ground cornmeal
1 tablespoon olive oil (optional)
1 teaspoon chopped sage or ¼ teaspoon dried sage
⅓ cup grated Parmesan cheese

In a 3-quart microwavable casserole, combine the milk, water, cornmeal, and olive oil, if desired, and sage. Cover tightly with a lid or vented plastic wrap. Microwave on HIGH for 5 minutes. Stir, re-cover, and microwave on HIGH for 4 to 6 minutes, or until thickened and most of the water is absorbed. Stir in the Parmesan cheese. Re-cover and let stand for 3 minutes.

Makes 4 servings

SOUTHERN GRITS CASSEROLE

Grits are probably the most popular Southern side dish. A high-fiber food, and good source of protein, grits can be enjoyed in both sweet and savory renditions. Note that stone-ground grits are definitely rougher in texture. Serve the Broccoli and Red Pepper Medley (page 148) as a colorful companion with this creamy dish.

2 tablespoons olive or vegetable oil
½ cup sliced scallions, including some green parts
1 small jalapeño pepper, finely diced, (optional)
3 cups water
1 cup grits
2 eggs, lightly beaten
2 cups grated sharp Cheddar cheese (8 ounces)
½ teaspoon freshly ground white pepper
Pinch ground red pepper

In a 3-quart microwavable casserole, combine the oil and scallions. Microwave on HIGH for 2 minutes. Stir in the water and grits. Cover tightly with a lid or vented plastic wrap. Microwave on HIGH for 8 to 12 minutes, or until thickened, stirring once. Add the eggs, cheese, pepper, and red pepper, and stir well to combine. Microwave on MEDIUM for 6 to 10 minutes, or until heated through and almost set. Let stand, covered, for 3 minutes.

Makes 4 servings as a main course, 6 to 8 servings as a side dish

RISOTTO WITH ASPARAGUS, MUSHROOMS, AND FONTINA

"No one can stop eating risotto; it goes down so easily," says Lorna J. Sass, noted food historian and pressure-cooker specialist. In this case you may understand why. If the forty-minute, hand-stirred risotto recipes are too tedious for you, this microwave version, which takes about half that time, might be just what you've been looking for. Italian Arborio rice is the most authentic but long-grain rice can be substituted.

1½ cups water
1 1-ounce package dried porcini mushrooms
1½ cups fresh asparagus pieces (1 inch)
3 tablespoons unsalted butter or olive oil
1 medium onion, coarsely chopped
1½ cups Italian Arborio rice
4 cups Basic Vegetable Stock (page 199) or Mushroom Stock (page 201)
⅔ cup Fontina cheese, cut into small pieces (3 ounces)
½ cup grated Parmesan cheese, or to taste
Salt and freshly ground black pepper to taste
2 tablespoons chopped parsley

Place water in a 4-cup glass measure and microwave on HIGH for 2 minutes, or until boiling. Stir in mushrooms and let soak for 10 minutes. Remove the mushrooms; chop coarsely and set aside. Reserve the liquid.

Put the asparagus in a small microwavable dish; sprinkle with 1 tablespoon water. Cover with vented plastic wrap. Microwave on HIGH for 1 minute. Uncover and set aside.

In a 3-quart microwavable casserole, combine the butter and onion. Microwave, uncovered, on HIGH for 2 minutes, or until the onion is tender. Add the rice and stir well to coat the grains with butter. Microwave on HIGH for 3 minutes longer.

Pour the stock and the reserved mushroom liquid into the rice mixture. Cover tightly with a lid or vented plastic wrap. Microwave on HIGH for 9 to 11 minutes or until boiling; stir and re-cover. Microwave on MEDIUM for 10 to 12 minutes or until most of the liquid is absorbed. The rice should remain firm to the bite and have a thick consistency. Stir in the mushrooms, asparagus, Fontina, and Parmesan cheese. Re-cover and let stand 5 minutes. Add salt and pepper to taste. Sprinkle with parsley and serve.

Makes 4 servings as a main course, 6 servings as an appetizer

RISOTTO WITH PEAS

Risi e bisi, the classic Venetian risotto, is as popular today as it was centuries ago. Fresh fennel, with its distinctive anise flavor, is added here to create a beautifully subtle dish. Finish it off with a generous grinding of fresh black pepper just before serving.

· ·

3 tablespoons olive oil
2 cups thinly sliced fennel bulb
⅓ cup finely chopped onion
½ teaspoon fennel seed
1½ cups Italian Arborio rice
4½ cups Basic Vegetable Stock (page 199)
½ cup dry white wine
2 cups fresh cooked peas or frozen tiny peas, defrosted (10-ounce package)
⅔ cup grated Parmesan cheese
Salt and freshly ground black pepper to taste
2 tablespoons chopped fennel leaves

· ·

In a 3-quart microwavable casserole, combine the oil, fennel, onion, and fennel seed. Cover tightly with a lid or vented plastic wrap. Microwave on HIGH for 3 minutes, or until the fennel is tender. Add the rice and stir well to coat the grains with butter. Microwave on HIGH for 3 minutes.

Pour the stock and wine into the rice mixture. Cover tightly with a lid or vented plastic wrap. Microwave on HIGH for 7 to 10 minutes, or until boiling; stir

(continued)

· ·

(continued)

and re-cover. Microwave on MEDIUM for 12 to 14 minutes, or until most of the liquid is absorbed. The rice should remain firm to the bite and have a thick consistency. Stir in the peas and Parmesan cheese. Re-cover and let stand for 5 minutes. Add salt and freshly ground black pepper to taste.

Garnish with chopped fennel leaves and serve.

Makes 4 servings as a main course, 6 servings as an appetizer

RISOTTO WITH BEANS

The combination of rice and beans is as favored in Italy as a high protein dish as it is in other parts of the world. When time permits, I like to use fresh navy beans but the canned variety would do just as well.

1½ cups cooked beans, (page 251) canned or drained
3 tablespoons olive oil
1 medium onion, coarsely chopped
1 medium tomato, coarsely chopped
1¼ cups Italian Arborio rice
4¾ cups Basic Vegetable Stock (page 199)
½ cup dry red or white wine
½ cup grated Romano cheese
2 tablespoons capers
3 to 4 tablespoons chopped basil or 2 teaspoons dried basil
Salt and freshly ground black pepper to taste

Place the beans in a 1-quart microwavable casserole. Cover tightly with a lid or vented plastic wrap. Microwave on HIGH for 2 minutes; set aside.

In a 3-quart microwavable casserole, combine the oil and onion. Cover tightly with a lid or vented plastic wrap. Microwave on HIGH for 2 minutes. Add the tomato. Re-cover and microwave on HIGH for 1 minute. Add the rice and stir well to coat the grains with oil. Re-cover and microwave on HIGH for 3 minutes.

Pour the stock and wine into the rice mixture. Re-cover and microwave on

HIGH for 9 to 11 minutes, or until boiling. Stir and re-cover. Microwave on MEDIUM for 9 to 11 minutes, or until most of the liquid is absorbed. The rice should remain firm to the bite and have a thick consistency. Stir in the beans, grated Romano, capers, and basil. Re-cover and let stand for 5 minutes. (If the beans are not at room temperature, you may want to cook on HIGH for 1 to 2 minutes before standing time, just to heat through.) And salt and pepper to taste.

Makes 4 servings as a main dish, 6 servings as an appetizer

TEMPEH AND NAPA STIR-FRY

Here's a recipe to try if you have a browning dish. Be sure to have a pair of oven mitts close by as the dish gets quite hot. Use a trivet or hot pad when placing it on a counter or tabletop.

Tempeh, the most important soy protein of Indonesia, is a pressed and fermented form of soybeans; it can also be made with seeds and grains. I like the kind mixed with millet, brown rice, and barley. It is available in most health-food stores in the refrigerated or frozen food section, and is very low in fat and cholesterol-free.

Napa cabbage, slightly sweeter than head cabbage, is a nice partner for tempeh. Serve this dish with hot cooked rice and pass extra rice vinegar and soy sauce for guests to add at the table.

Try to leave the dish in the oven as much as possible between steps so it doesn't cool down too much.

2 tablespoons sesame oil
8 ounces tempeh, cut in ½-inch cubes
¼ cup rice vinegar
1½ tablespoons Tamari or soy sauce
¼ teaspoon crushed red pepper, or to taste
5 cups shredded Napa cabbage
1 cup shredded spinach leaves
1 cup bean sprouts

(continued)

(continued)

Prepare the browning dish according to the manufacturer's instructions.

Pour the oil into the dish. Add the tempeh and stir briefly just to coat with oil. Microwave on HIGH for 7 minutes, stirring once.

Meanwhile, in a 1-cup glass measure, combine the vinegar, Tamari, and pepper.

Add the cabbage, spinach, and bean sprouts to the browning dish. Pour the vinegar mixture over the top. Microwave on HIGH for 4 to 6 minutes, or until the cabbage is tender-crisp stirring once.

Serve immediately.

Makes 2 to 3 servings

VIETNAMESE PHO

Wait until you have fresh vegetable and mushroom stocks to make this recipe; canned or dehydrated ones just don't do the job. Traditionally served with beef, herbs, and bean sprouts, this "soup" presents well as a main dish. I sometimes serve it with chunks of tofu to replace the protein of the meat.

6 cups Basic Vegetable Stock (page 199)
6 cups Mushroom Stock (page 201)
1 large onion, thinly sliced
6 quarter-size pieces fresh ginger
1 stalk fresh lemon grass, trimmed, or peel of 1 lemon, yellow part only
1 cinnamon stick (about 3 inches)
8 black peppercorns
Bibb lettuce leaves
1½ cups bean sprouts
½ cup each tightly packed cilantro, basil, and mint leaves, shredded
3 scallions, thinly sliced, including green parts
2 large jalapeño peppers, thinly sliced
2 small limes, cut into wedges
¼ cup red chili paste

¾ pound dry rice noodles or thin spaghetti, cooked with 2 tablespoons
   vegetable oil and drained
1 pound firm tofu, pressed dry and cut into ½-inch pieces

In a 5-quart microwavable casserole, combine the vegetable and mushroom stocks, onion, ginger, lemon grass, cinnamon stick, and peppercorns. Cover with a lid or vented plastic wrap. Microwave on HIGH for 10 to 12 minutes, or until boiling. Stir and partially re-cover. Microwave on MEDIUM for 20 to 30 minutes to develop flavor. Rotate the casserole once during cooking. Let stand, covered, for 10 minutes.

Meanwhile, arrange the lettuce leaves on a large serving platter. Mound bean sprouts in the center; surround with separate piles of cilantro, basil, mint leaves, and scallions. Place pepper slices on top of the sprouts and lime wedges around the outside of the platter. Spoon the chili paste into a small serving dish.

Strain the broth into a microwavable bowl or casserole, gently pressing the liquid out of the onion and spices with the back of a spoon. Discard the seasonings. If necessary, microwave the broth on HIGH for 2 minutes to reheat. Divide the noodles and tofu equally into 6 deep soup bowls; ladle hot broth on the top.

Pass the sprouts and herbs at the table for your guests to add as desired.

Makes 6 to 8 servings

N O T E : A quick method for pressed tofu is to wrap it in a kitchen towel, then place a heavy dish or jar on top. Refrigerate for about 1 hour, or until firm. Unwrap and slice.

THAI VEGETABLE CURRY

If you like a fiery curry this recipe will truly delight you. The recipe is an adaptation from Barbara Hansen's *Taste of Southeast Asia*. This book, like her others, is wonderfully researched and clearly written. Each of the recipes is a treasure.

3 14-ounce cans coconut milk (4 cups)
¼ cup green or red curry paste (see Note)
½ pound green beans, trimmed and cut into 1½-inch pieces
1 cup frozen tiny peas, defrosted and drained
1 15-ounce can straw mushrooms, drained
1 15-ounce can baby corn, drained
4 ounces firm tofu, pressed dry (pages 116–117) and cut into 1-inch cubes
1 cup lightly packed basil leaves
1 jalapeño pepper, cut into thin strips (optional)
1 teaspoon sugar (optional)
3 cups cooked brown rice (page 260)

Measure ½ cup of the thickest milk from the top of a can of coconut milk (do not shake beforehand) into a 3-quart microwavable casserole. Pour 3½ cups of the remaining coconut milk into a 4-cup glass measure and set aside.)

Microwave the thick coconut milk on MEDIUM-HIGH for 1 minute. Stir in curry paste until well blended. Microwave on MEDIUM for 4 to 6 minutes, or until oil separates from the curry paste, stirring every 2 minutes. Stir in the remaining coconut milk. Microwave on HIGH for 2 to 4 minutes, or until the mixture is very hot but not boiling; add green beans. Cover with a lid or vented plastic wrap. Microwave on HIGH for 5 minutes. Reduce setting to MEDIUM for 8 to 10 minutes, or until the green beans are tender. (The mixture should be just simmering, not boiling, or it will separate. Cook on MEDIUM-LOW, if necessary to avoid this.) Stir in the peas, mushrooms, corn, tofu, and basil leaves, and the jalapeño pepper and sugar if desired. Re-cover and microwave on HIGH for 3 minutes, or until heated through. Let stand for 10 minutes.

Spoon into a serving bowl over hot cooked rice.

Makes 4 to 6 servings

．．

NOTE: Some curry pastes contain a small amount of shrimp paste. Check ingredient labels carefully before purchasing if you are a very strict vegetarian and want to avoid this. You can also make your own curry paste (see page 227).

TOFU AND CELLOPHANE NOODLE SALAD

Cellophane noodles are readily available in supermarkets and Oriental food stores, so it's easy to enjoy them on a regular basis. I recommend using Tamari, a dark full-bodied, and mellow soy sauce. It contains only soy, salt, and water not corn syrup, colorings, or other additions frequently found in soy sauce.

．．

½ cup lemon juice
¼ cup chopped cilantro, divided
1 to 2 serrano or jalapeño peppers to taste, finely chopped
3 tablespoons chopped ginger
2 tablespoons Tamari or soy sauce, or to taste
2 teaspoons rice wine vinegar, or to taste
1 tablespoon water
10½ ounces extra firm tofu, drained and cut into 1-inch cubes (see Note)
1 3¾ ounces package cellophane noodles
2 cups water
½ pound snow peas, trimmed
2 tablespoons water
½ cup chopped red bell pepper
½ cup thinly sliced red onion
Bibb lettuce leaves
1 large tomato, sliced

．．

In a large nonmetallic mixing bowl, combine the lemon juice, 2 tablespoons of the cilantro, the peppers, ginger, Tamari, vinegar, and water. Add the tofu and stir until combined. Cover and refrigerate for several hours or overnight.

Place noodles in a large nonmetallic bowl. Pour water into a 2-cup glass measure and microwave on HIGH for 2 minutes, or until boiling. Pour the water over

(continued)

．．

(continued)

the noodles. Soak for 15 minutes, or until soft; drain and set aside. (If noodles are not completely softened, place the bowl in the microwave and cook on HIGH for 3 to 5 minutes, or until the noodles are clear, stirring once.)

Place snow peas in a 1-quart microwavable casserole. Sprinkle with 2 tablespoons water. Cover with vented plastic wrap and microwave on HIGH for 1 minute. Let stand, covered, for 2 minutes. Cut snow peas into 1-inch pieces. Add snow peas, bell pepper, and onion to the noodles; toss to combine. Add the dressing with the tofu; toss gently. Add more Tamari or vinegar, if desired.

Arrange the lettuce on a serving platter. Place the tomato slices in a circle around the edge. Top with the noodle mixture. Sprinkle with the remaining cilantro.

Makes 6 servings

NOTE: Mori-Nu now makes silken tofu "extra-firm." Alternately, you can press tofu as directed on pages 116–117.

ASIAN NOODLE SALAD

Spicy Peanut Sauce is so versatile and nice to keep on hand. I often use it as a dip, and I find it is great tossed with cooked noodles and vegetables.

1 8-ounce package Japanese wheat noodles (udon) or thin fettuccine, cooked
2 to 3 tablespoons sesame oil
½ pound fresh broccoli
1 small carrot, peeled and cut into 1 × ⅛-inch strips (about ½ cup)
½ medium red bell pepper, seeded and cut into 1 × ⅛-inch strips
2 scallions
1½ cups bean sprouts
1 cup Spicy Peanut Sauce (page 207)
1 tablespoon Tamari or soy sauce
Romaine lettuce leaves (optional)
1 tablespoon toasted sesame seeds
Crushed red pepper
Soy sauce or Tamari

In a large mixing bowl, toss the cooked noodles with the oil; set aside.

Separate the broccoli into 1-inch florets (you should have about 2 cups); reserve the stalks for another purpose. Place the broccoli around the edge of a 12-inch round glass platter. Arrange the carrot and pepper strips in the center of the plate in a single layer. Thinly slice the white parts of the scallions and sprinkle them over the top of the vegetables. (Slice the green tops, saving about 2 tablespoons for garnish.) Cover the platter with vented plastic wrap. Microwave on HIGH for 2 to 3 minutes, or until the vegetables are tender-crisp. Let stand, covered, for 1 minute.

Toss the vegetables and bean sprouts with the noodles. Add the peanut sauce (thinned with water or stock, if necessary) and Tamari; toss to coat. If desired, place the lettuce leaves on a serving platter and arrange the noodles in the center. Sprinkle with reserved scallions and sesame seeds.

Serve at room temperature with crushed red pepper and soy sauce on the side.

Makes 4 servings

SUSHI

The Japanese dish called *sushi*, or *norimaki*, is becoming very popular in the United States. Few dishes are as eye-catching and have such good flavor and nutritive value. With a couple of basic ingredients and a good sharp knife, anyone can be serving up sushi in no time flat. In fact, the recipe (which is divided into steps) appears longer than the actual time it takes.

You can let your imagination go wild and use just about any combination of vegetables and grains. I like to alternate brown, white, and wild rice for the base. A variety of vegetables can be steamed on a single platter, making blanching a thing of the past. And as the rice cooks in the microwave you can be making up fillings and dipping sauces. When you are ready to serve, arrange the sliced sushi on a lacquered tray or platter with soy sauce and dipping sauce, and watercress sprigs for garnish.

4 whole toasted nori (seaweed) sheets
Rice (see right)
Wasabi or Umeboshi Flavoring Paste (see right) or spicy mustard
Fillings (see page 124)
Lime-Ginger or Mirin Dipping Sauce (see pages 124–125) or soy sauce

Place a sheet of nori, shiny side down, on a bamboo rolling mat. Wet your hands, or the back of a spoon, and gently pat a heaping ½ cup of rice over the nori. The rice layer should be about ¼ inch thick, leaving a ½-inch strip across the top uncovered. Spread about 1 teaspoon of flavoring paste or spicy mustard in a thin line 1 inch from the bottom of the rice. Just above the line, with a dampened finger, make a small indentation across the rice. Arrange 2 or 3 fillings in it. Mix colors for contrast; for instance, try a tofu and red pepper strip with a few basil leaves.

Starting at the bottom, grasp the edges of the mat and roll tightly with even pressure to form a cylinder. Squeeze gently to avoid bulges and to make an even roll. Lightly moisten the top outer edge and press to seal the roll. Using a sharp, wet knife, slice each roll into about 6 pieces, occasionally wiping the knife with a wet towel. Serve with soy sauce and dipping sauce.

RICE
. . . .

3 cups cooked short-grain brown or white rice, warm (page 260)
2 tablespoons rice wine vinegar
1 tablespoon sugar
2 teaspoons mirin or dry sherry
¼ teaspoon salt

. . . .

Turn the rice out onto a large nonmetallic platter. In a small bowl, mix together the vinegar, sugar, mirin, and salt. Sprinkle over the rice and toss well to combine. Spread rice out over the platter and let cool.

WASABI FLAVORING PASTES
. . . .

2 teaspoons wasabi powder (Japanese horseradish)
1 tablespoon water

. . . .

In a small bowl, combine the wasabi and water to form a smooth paste.

UMEBOSHI FLAVORING PASTE
. . . .

2 tablespoons umeboshi paste (pickled plum)
2 tablespoons tahini
Water to thin

. . . .

In a small bowl, combine the umeboshi paste, tahini, and 1 to 2 tablespoons of water to make a thick, smooth paste.

(continued)

. . . .

(continued)

FILLINGS
••••••••

½ medium red or yellow bell pepper, seeded and cut into julienne strips,
   about 4 inches long
½ medium carrot, peeled and cut into julienne strips
4 scallions, green parts only, about 4 inches long
4 large spinach leaves, washed, stems removed, and cut into 1-inch strips
4 large basil leaves, shredded
1 slice firm tofu, pressed dry (pages 116–117) and cut into ¼-inch strips

On a 12-inch round paper or microwavable plate, arrange the pepper and carrot strips in a layer around the outside of the plate. In the center, arrange separate piles of scallions, spinach, and basil leaves. Cover loosely with vented plastic wrap. Microwave on HIGH for 1 to 1½ minutes, or until the vegetables are tender. Let stand, covered, for 1 minute. Remove the wrap and drain excess water.

LIME-GINGER DIPPING SAUCE
•••••••••••••••••••••••

2 tablespoons fresh lime juice
2 tablespoons soy sauce
2 teaspoons grated fresh ginger

In a small bowl, combine the lime juice, soy sauce, and ginger.

MIRIN DIPPING SAUCE
••••••••••••••••••

2 tablespoons mirin or dry sherry
2 tablespoons rice vinegar

In a small bowl, combine the mirin and vinegar.

Makes 20 to 24 pieces

NOTE: All of the ingredients are available at health-food stores and Japanese markets.

VEGETARIAN PAELLA

Chunks of fresh corn on the cob give the paella a real substantial feeling. With this basic recipe, feel free to add green beans, limas, carrots, or chick peas. Without all the usual oven heat, I've made this for company on summer nights in Los Angeles and stayed cool all the while.

¼ cup olive oil
2 medium onions, thinly sliced
4 garlic cloves, minced
1 large red or green bell pepper, seeded and sliced into 1 × ½-inch strips
2 cups short-grain brown or white rice
½ teaspoon saffron threads, soaked in ½ cup hot water
3½ to 4½ cups Basic Vegetable Stock (page 199)
2 medium tomatoes, chopped
1 celery rib, with leaves, chopped
1 bay leaf
2 medium ears fresh corn, husked and cut into 1½-inch pieces
1 cup frozen tiny peas, defrosted
½ cup sliced black olives
3 tablespoons chopped parsley
Salt and freshly ground black pepper to taste
½ cup toasted slivered almonds, for garnish (optional)

(continued)

(continued)

In a 5-quart microwavable casserole or baking dish, combine the oil, onions, and garlic. Microwave on HIGH for 4 to 6 minutes, or until the onion is tender. Add the pepper and rice; toss well to coat with oil. Microwave on HIGH for 6 minutes, stirring once. Stir in the saffron and water, 3½ cups of the stock, the tomatoes, celery, bay leaf, and corn. Cover tightly with a lid or vented plastic wrap. Microwave on HIGH for 15 to 19 minutes, or until boiling. Stir and re-cover. Microwave on MEDIUM for 55 to 65 minutes, or until the rice is tender and most of the liquid is absorbed. Stir in the peas, olives, and parsley. Cover tightly with a lid or vented plastic wrap and let stand, for 10 minutes. Add salt and pepper to taste. Garnish with slivered almonds, if desired.

Makes 6 servings

N O T E : Add additional stock, if necessary, during the simmering phase (MEDIUM setting) or to reheat leftovers as the paella will thicken considerably on standing.

JOB'S MULTIGRAIN CASSEROLE

Job's Tears is an esteemed new grain that has actually been around for centuries. Also known as Hato Mugi Barley, it has a good nutritional profile and is high in protein. The multigrain mix is a nice complement to it and actually smoothes out the "grassy" flavor that Job's Tears tends to have. The Eden brand of Job's Tears is nationally available in many health-food stores. I am quite fond of the Neshaminy Valley dry chestnuts which are also available in health-food stores. You could use canned or bottled ones as well. When cooked, the chestnuts will break up into sweet, crunchy nuggets. Remember that chestnuts are very low in fat yet rich in flavor and carbohydrates.

1 medium onion, coarsely chopped
1 medium carrot, coarsely chopped
2 tablespoons canola oil
1 large celery rib, cut on a wide diagonal
3½ cups Basic Vegetable Stock (page 199) or Mushroom Stock (page 201)

½ cup dry white wine
¾ cup Job's Tear, rinsed and drained
⅓ cup dried or ⅔ cup canned chestnuts, drained
½ cup Multigrain Mix (page 229)
½ cup chopped chervil or 2½ tablespoons dried, divided
1 tablespoon chopped celery leaves
Salt and freshly ground white pepper to taste

In a 1-quart microwavable casserole, combine the onion, carrot, and oil. Cover tightly with a lid or vented plastic wrap. Microwave on HIGH for 2 minutes. Stir in the celery. Re-cover and microwave for 1 minute longer; set aside.

In a 3-quart oval casserole, combine the stock, wine, Job's Tear, and chestnuts. Cover tightly with a lid or vented plastic wrap. Microwave on HIGH for 15 minutes. Stir in the reserved vegetables, multigrain mix, ¼ cup of the chervil and the celery leaves. Re-cover and microwave on MEDIUM-HIGH for 50 to 60 minutes, or until the grains are tender. (Add additional stock or water if the casserole seems a bit dry.)

Using the back of a large fork or serving spoon to break up the chestnuts, stir in the remaining chervil, and add salt and pepper to taste. Re-cover and let stand for 10 minutes.

Makes 4 servings

RATATOUILLE

Use a variety of colors—red, yellow, and green—for the peppers, if you can. The final result is beautiful. Ratatouille is best when made a day or two ahead. Leftover, it is great as a side dish or in a sandwich. A dollop of yogurt is a nice complement whether you're serving this dish hot or cold.

¼ cup olive oil
1 large onion, sliced
2 large garlic cloves, minced
1 medium eggplant, cut into 1-inch cubes (about 1 pound)
½ pound bell peppers, red, yellow, green, or mixed, seeded and cut into 1 × ½-inch strips
1 medium zucchini or yellow squash, cut into ½-inch slices (about 6 ounces)
3 Italian plum tomatoes, cored and cut into quarters
⅓ cup red wine or ¼ cup balsamic vinegar
1 tablespoon chopped basil or 1½ teaspoons dried basil
1 tablespoon oregano or 1½ teaspoons dried oregano
½ teaspoon anise or fennel seeds, crushed
¼ teaspoon freshly ground black pepper
1 bay leaf
Salt to taste

In a 3-quart microwavable casserole, combine the oil, onion, and garlic. Microwave on HIGH for 1 minute. Stir in the eggplant, tossing well to coat with oil. Cover tightly with a lid or vented plastic wrap. Microwave on HIGH for 3 to 5 minutes, or until the eggplant is just tender.

Stir in the pepper strips, zucchini, tomatoes, wine, basil, oregano, anise seeds, pepper, and bay leaf. Re-cover and microwave on HIGH for 10 to 12 minutes, or until the vegetables are tender; stir and rotate once. Let stand, covered, for 10 minutes. Remove bay leaf. Add salt to taste.

Serve hot or at room temperature. Store leftovers, covered, in a nonmetallic container in the refrigerator.

Makes 3 to 4 servings as a main dish, 6 to 8 servings as a side dish

. . . .

NOTE: This is a crisper version of ratatouille than most. If you prefer it softer, reduce setting to MEDIUM and continue to cook for 10 to 15 minutes.

VEGETABLE KABOBS

Marinate the vegetables on their skewers for several hours or overnight, if you have the time. (Dampen wooden or bamboo skewers with water or brush them lightly with oil to prevent sticking.) If there's an excellent bottled dressing on your shelf, use that instead of my marinade for ultimate convenience. Steamed rice or bulgur is an easy accompaniment. I like to pass a Spicy Peanut Sauce (page 207) as a final touch.

. . . .

2 tablespoons olive oil
1 teaspoon lemon juice
1 teaspoon dry mustard
2 tablespoons chopped chives
¼ teaspoon freshly ground black pepper
2 small green or yellow squash, cut into 1-inch slices (about 10 ounces)
8 medium whole mushrooms, washed and trimmed
1 large green or red bell pepper, seeded and cut into 1½-inch squares
8 cherry tomatoes
½ pound firm tofu, pressed dry (pages 116–117) and cut into 1-inch cubes

. . . .

In a small bowl, combine the olive oil, lemon juice, mustard, chives, and pepper.

Thread the vegetables on each of 8 skewers as follows: a slice of squash, mushroom, pepper, tomato, and tofu. Place skewers like spokes of a wheel on a 12-inch round microwavable platter; brush each with half of the marinade. If possible, let stand for several hours, covered, at room temperature.

Microwave on HIGH for 3 minutes. Turn and move skewers so that the inside tip is now on the outside. Brush again with the marinade. Microwave on HIGH for another 3 minutes, or until the squash is tender-crisp.

Makes 4 servings

. . . .

CAULIFLOWER STEW

Broccoli, tomato, and tofu team up with cauliflower for an easy stew. Toss in some crushed red pepper with the tofu if you like foods as spicy as I do. A grain pilaf and tossed salad combined with this stew make an effortless meal.

¼ cup peanut oil
4 garlic cloves, minced
3 tablespoons chopped ginger
1 small onion, thinly sliced
½ teaspoon ground turmeric
1 small cauliflower, cut into 1-inch pieces (about 1 pound)
2 cups broccoli florets, cut about 1½ inches long
1 medium tomato, coarsely chopped
⅔ cup Basic Vegetable Stock (page 199) or water
2 tablespoons dry sherry (optional)
2 teaspoons soy sauce, or to taste
1 10½-ounce package extra-firm tofu, drained and cut into 1-inch cubes

In a 5-quart microwavable casserole, combine the oil, garlic, ginger, onion, and turmeric. Microwave on HIGH for 2 minutes. Add the cauliflower, stirring well to coat with oil. Microwave on HIGH for 6 minutes. Stir in the broccoli and microwave on HIGH for 3 minutes. Add the tomato, stock, dry sherry if desired, and soy sauce; stir to combine. Cover tightly with a lid or vented plastic wrap. Microwave on HIGH for 9 to 14 minutes, or until the vegetables are tender (longer if you prefer softer vegetables), stirring once.

Gently stir in the tofu. Re-cover and microwave on HIGH for 1 minute. Let stand, covered, for 10 minutes.

Makes 4 to 6 servings

STUFFED ACORN SQUASH

There's almost no end to the possibilities for stuffing for acorn squash. This high-fiber, vitamin A–packed vegetable is as adaptable as can be. Here I used the Multigrain Pilaf with some fresh papaya and tarragon added to make a bright entree. You can also add currants or prunes and some nuts. The Three-Bread Stuffing (pages 134–135) is another good choice, as are cranberries and apples if you like a fruit filling.

2 medium acorn squash (about 1¼ pounds each)
2 cups cooked Multigrain Pilaf (page 167)
⅔ cup diced papaya
1 tablespoon chopped tarragon or 1 teaspoon dried tarragon
Salt and freshly ground black pepper to taste

Pierce each squash in 3 to 4 places with the tip of a sharp knife. Place them on a double layer of paper towels on the floor of the oven. Microwave on HIGH for 8 minutes, or until just soft to the touch, rotating once during cooking. Let stand for 5 minutes.

Meanwhile, in a medium bowl, combine the pilaf, papaya, and tarragon. (If you are using leftover pilaf that has been in the refrigerator, place it in a 1-quart microwavable dish, cover, and microwave on HIGH for 1 to 2 minutes, or until heated through.) Taste the mixture and adjust the seasonings, adding salt and pepper to taste.

Cut each squash in half and scoop out the seeds. Spoon ¼ of the pilaf mixture into each of the shells. Place the filled halves on a 12-inch round glass plate. Cover loosely with wax paper or vented plastic wrap. Microwave on HIGH for 4 to 6 minutes, or until heated through. Let stand, covered, for 2 minutes.

Makes 4 servings

STUFFED CHAYOTE

Chayote is a Latin American summer squash that was grown by the Aztecs and Mayans centuries ago. It's only natural then that it be teamed up with quinoa, the ancient Peruvian grain. Leave the seeds in while cooking; they're edible when finished.

2 tablespoons water
2 large chayote, cut in half lengthwise (about ¾ pound each)
2 tablespoons olive oil
2 garlic cloves, minced
½ cup finely chopped onion
⅓ cup finely chopped celery
1 medium tomato, peeled and chopped
3 tablespoons chopped parsley, divided
½ teaspoon ground allspice
¼ teaspoon freshly ground black pepper
¾ cup cooked quinoa (page 260)
Chayote seeds, chopped (optional)
1 tablespoon dry red wine or balsamic vinegar

Place the water in an 11 × 7-inch microwavable baking dish. Place chayote, cut side down, with widest part of the squash on the outside of the dish. Cover with vented plastic wrap. Microwave on HIGH for 8 to 10 minutes, or until just tender, turning the chayote over and rotating the dish after 3 minutes. Let stand, covered, for 5 minutes. Uncover and set aside to cool.

In a 1-quart microwavable casserole, combine the oil, garlic, onion, and celery, tossing well to coat. Microwave on HIGH for 2 to 3 minutes, or until the onion is tender.

Using a large spoon, gently scoop out the chayote pulp onto a double layer of paper towels to absorb water, leaving a ¼-inch-thick shell. Blot excess water from the shell if necessary. Chop pulp; add to the onion mixture. Stir in the tomato, 2 tablespoons of the parsley, allspice, and pepper. Microwave on HIGH for 4 minutes, stirring once during cooking. Stir in quinoa, chopped chayote seeds, if desired, and wine or vinegar.

Spoon the filling into the chayote halves and place in an 11 × 7-inch baking dish. Microwave on HIGH for 4 minutes or until heated through. Sprinkle with remaining parsley.

Makes 4 servings

STUFFED PEPPERS

I was going to bypass this recipe, but there were all sorts of complaints from my friends: "What, no recipe for stuffed peppers?" So here it is. There are so many ways to do this, you can make it once a week and never have it be the same twice. The vibrant colors of peppers on the market alone make a big difference. Rice is pretty much a classic for stuffing peppers, but any cooked grain—millet, quinoa, bulgur—is fine. Chopped pecans lend crunch and extra richness for a fine main dish. Spicy Corn Bread (page 68) and steamed broccoli complete the meal.

4 medium bell peppers, yellow, green, or red (about 6 ounces each)
2 tablespoons olive oil
¼ cup finely chopped scallions, white parts only
1 celery rib, finely chopped
2 cups cooked brown rice
1 medium tomato, seeded and chopped
⅓ cup chopped pecans
¼ cup oil-cured olives, pitted and finely chopped
3 tablespoons finely chopped parsley
1 teaspoon chopped oregano or ½ teaspoon dried oregano
1 teaspoon chopped basil or ½ teaspoon dried basil
½ teaspoon freshly ground black pepper
2 tablespoons water
2 cups tomato sauce (optional)
Chopped parsley, for garnish

(continued)

(continued)

Slice the tops off the peppers and remove their seeds and membranes. Wash the peppers and set them upside down on a paper towel to drain.

In a 10-inch glass pie plate or 2-quart shallow round microwavable casserole, combine the oil, scallions, and celery. Microwave on HIGH for 1 minute. Stir in the rice, tomato, pecans, olives, parsley, oregano, basil, and pepper. Spoon the mixture evenly into the hollowed-out peppers and place them back in the dish, arranged in a circle. Pour water in the bottom of the dish.

Cover lightly with vented plastic wrap. Microwave on HIGH for 6 minutes. Rotate the dish half a turn. Microwave on MEDIUM for 6 to 8 minutes, or until the peppers are tender when pierced with the tip of a sharp knife. Let stand, covered, for 5 minutes.

If desired, pour some tomato sauce onto a serving platter. Set the peppers on top and serve with additional sauce, garnished with chopped parsley.

Makes 4 servings

THREE-BREAD STUFFING

Does stuffing always have to be a side dish? This one is just so satisfying I could take it as is anyday with perhaps a salad and a vegetable dish. I deliberately leave the seeds in the jalapeño pepper for a spicier stuffing. Use any trio of your favorite breads, perhaps adding some chopped prunes and pecans to the basic recipe.

½ pound rye bread, cut into 1-inch cubes
½ pound pumpernickel bread, cut into 1-inch cubes
½ pound sourdough bread, cut into 1-inch cubes
¼ cup peanut oil
¼ cup unsalted butter
2 celery ribs, coarsely chopped
1 large onion, coarsely chopped
1 medium Granny Smith apple, cored and coarsely chopped
1 jalapeño pepper, seeded and finely chopped

3 tablespoons chopped parsley
1 teaspoon caraway seeds
½ teaspoon salt
½ teaspoon freshly ground black pepper
¼ teaspoon crushed red pepper (optional)
2 cups Basic Vegetable Stock (page 199)
2 eggs, lightly beaten

Place bread cubes in a large shallow pan. Let them dry out for several hours or overnight.

In a 2½-quart oval casserole, combine the oil, butter, celery, and onion. Microwave on HIGH for 2 to 3 minutes, or until the onion is tender. Stir in the apple and jalapeño pepper. Microwave on HIGH for 1 minute.

In a large mixing bowl, combine the bread cubes with the cooked celery-apple mixture. Stir in the parsley, caraway seeds, salt, pepper, crushed red pepper, if desired, stock, and eggs. Mix until thoroughly combined.

Spoon stuffing into the casserole, smoothing the top. Cover loosely with plastic wrap or wax paper. Microwave on HIGH for 10 to 12 minutes, or until heated through, rotating once during cooking. Let stand, covered, for 5 minutes.

Makes 8 servings

MAIN MEAL-STUFFED POTATOES

After popcorn, baked potatoes are the most frequently microwaved food! Most microwave owners have already mastered baking potatoes, so why not transform them into a vegetarian main dish? Substitute any of your favorite vegetables, leftover chili, or ratatouille for the stuffing.

4 baking potatoes (8 ounces each), scrubbed
1½ cups low-fat cottage cheese
½ cup plain yogurt
1 cup cooked or canned corn
2 scallions, white parts only, thinly sliced
½ medium red bell pepper, seeded and diced
3 tablespoons chopped chives
Salt and freshly ground black pepper to taste
2 tablespoons chopped parsley

Pierce potatoes with a fork. Place on a double layer of paper towels in a circle on the floor of the oven, leaving about 1 inch between potatoes. Microwave on HIGH for 12 to 15 minutes, or until just tender, turning once during cooking. Let stand for 5 to 10 minutes.

Meanwhile, in a large mixing bowl, combine the cottage cheese, yogurt, corn, scallions, bell pepper, and chives. Cut the potatoes in half lengthwise and scoop out the flesh into the mixing bowl, leaving a ¼-inch thick shells. Stir thoroughly to combine; add salt and pepper to taste

Fill the potato shells with the mixture and place on a 12-inch round microwavable plate. Microwave on HIGH for 8 to 10 minutes. Let stand for 3 minutes. Sprinkle with parsley and serve.

Makes 4 servings

ORIENTAL STUFFED POTATOES

Dinner for two in minutes is what this recipe is about. Serve potatoes with a mixed vegetable side dish and a bean-sprout salad to complete the meal. If you're really in a hurry, split the potatoes, squeeze gently to fluff them and top with the tofu mixture.

2 baking potatoes (8 ounces each), scrubbed
4 ounces extra-firm tofu, cut into ½-inch pieces
1 tablespoon lemon juice
2 teaspoons sesame oil
2 teaspoons soy sauce or Tamari
1 teaspoon toasted sesame seeds
Shichimi togarashi (red pepper mix), see Note (optional)

Pierce potatoes with a fork. Place on a double layer of paper towels on the floor of the oven. Microwave on HIGH for 8 to 10 minutes, or until just tender, turning once during cooking. Let stand for 5 minutes.

Meanwhile, in a medium bowl, combine the tofu, lemon juice, sesame oil, and soy sauce. Cut the potatoes in half lengthwise and scoop out the flesh into the mixing bowl, leaving ¼-inch shells. Stir the ingredients in the bowl thoroughly to combine.

Fill the potato shells with the mixture and place on a 12-inch round microwavable plate. Microwave on HIGH for 3 to 4 minutes, or until heated through. Sprinkle with sesame seeds and shichimi togarashi, if desired.

Makes 2 servings

N O T E : Shichimi togarashi is a Japanese blend that includes red pepper, sesame seed, seaweed, orange peel, and mulberry. It is available in Asian markets and many supermarkets.

STUFFED EGGPLANT

Orzo are pearly grains of pasta that bear a striking resemblance to rice. Popular in Greek cooking, orzo is a perfect ingredient for any stuffed vegetable.

2 medium eggplants (about 12 ounces each)
Salt
3 tablespoons olive oil
2 scallions, white parts with 1 inch of green parts, thinly sliced
1 medium tomato, diced
1 cup cooked orzo, slightly underdone
2 tablespoons raisins
2 tablespoons toasted pine nuts
2 tablespoons chopped parsley
1 teaspoon dried thyme
1 teaspoon dried oregano
½ teaspoon salt
¼ teaspoon freshly ground black pepper

Wash the eggplants, remove the stems and cut each in half lengthwise. Score each fleshy side diagonally. Sprinkle with salt and let stand for 30 minutes. Scoop out the pulp leaving ¼-inch thick shells; coarsely chop the pulp into ¼-inch pieces. Sprinkle the shells with salt. Turn over onto a paper towel to drain.

In 3-quart microwavable casserole, combine 1 tablespoon of the oil and the scallions. Microwave on HIGH for 1 minute. Add the remaining oil and the eggplant pulp, tossing well to coat with oil. Microwave on HIGH for 4 to 7 minutes, or until the eggplant is tender.

Stir in the tomato, orzo, raisins, pine nuts, parsley, thyme, oregano, salt, and pepper, mixing well to combine. Spoon the filling into the eggplant shells.

Place the shells on a 12-inch round glass plate, thick ends toward the outside of the plate. Cover loosely with plastic wrap or wax paper. Microwave on HIGH for 11 to 13 minutes, or until eggplants are tender, rearranging after 8 minutes. Let stand, covered, for 5 minutes.

Makes 4 servings

N O T E : Salting eggplant before cooking not only draws out bitter flavor, but it actually prevents the eggplant from absorbing excess oil. In any recipe salt and drain the eggplant cubes, then blot or press dry with a paper towel before cooking.

ZUCCHINI-CORN STRATA

The ultimate prepared-in-advance dish, a strata is merely layers of bread cubes, grated cheese, vegetables, herbs, and spices, topped with seasoned eggs and milk. Create your own masterpiece using whatever bread, cheese, or other filling ingredient strikes your fancy. That also means you can serve the strata for breakfast, lunch, or dinner. Before cooking, let it chill for eight to twenty-four hours so it is moist and creamy throughout.

2 tablespoons olive oil
1 cup thinly sliced mushrooms
½ cup diced red bell pepper
¼ cup chopped celery
3 scallions, thinly sliced
6 slices seven-grain bread, crusts removed and cut into 1-inch cubes
2 cups shredded mozzarella cheese (8 ounces)
2 cups thinly sliced zucchini
1 cup fresh or canned, drained corn kernels
4 eggs
2 cups milk
2 tablespoons Dijon mustard
¾ teaspoon freshly ground black pepper
½ teaspoon salt
½ teaspoon ground nutmeg

In a 3-quart oval microwavable casserole or 11 × 7-inch baking dish, combine the oil, mushrooms, pepper, celery, and scallions. Stir well to coat with oil. Micro-

(continued)

wave on HIGH for 2 minutes. Transfer the mixture to a small dish. Add additional oil to the casserole, if necessary, so that the bottom and sides are lightly greased.

Place about half the bread cubes in the bottom of the casserole and sprinkle half the cheese on top. Spoon the mushroom mixture over the cheese, then arrange the zucchini and corn on top, layering 1 cup of the zucchini, all the corn, and then the remaining zucchini. Cover with the remaining bread cubes and cheese.

In a medium bowl, beat the eggs, milk, mustard, salt, pepper and nutmeg until blended. Ladle over the casserole. Cover tightly with a lid or plastic wrap and refrigerate for 8 to 24 hours.

Uncover the casserole and microwave on MEDIUM-HIGH for 30 to 35 minutes, or until set and heated through. Rotate the casserole after 15 minutes. Use a rubber spatula or fork and gently insert it around the edges to release the egg mixture for even cooking. Let stand for 5 minutes.

Makes 6 servings

VARIATIONS : *Bread*—Whole wheat, dark pumpernickel, rye, sourdough, corn, buttermilk, brioche, croissants, and tortillas. *Cheese*—Swiss, Fontina, Havarti, Munster, Cheddar, Provolone, Monterey Jack, Gruyère, and Jarlsberg. *Vegetables*— broccoli, spinach, potatoes, wild mushrooms, tomatoes, carrots, onions, parsnips, and snow peas. *Seasonings*—chilies, barbecue sauce, Worcestershire sauce, onions, tarragon, basil, chives, thyme, and dry mustard.

CHEESE ENCHILADAS

In addition to being an expert on Southeast Asian cuisine, Barbara Hansen is a master of Mexican foods. Inspired by the "deluxe" enchilada recipe in her *Mexican Cooking* book, this vegetarian version is quite special. Use canned enchilada sauce in place of the tomatillo one here for a shortcut.

1 13-ounce can tomatillos, drained or one 14-ounce can whole tomatoes, drained
½ cup yogurt or sour cream

½ cup cottage cheese
¼ cup cilantro leaves
1 tablespoon canola oil
1 large onion, coarsely chopped
1 4-ounce can chopped chilies, drained
2½ cups grated Monterey Jack or Cheddar cheese (10 ounces)
¼ teaspoon freshly ground white pepper
8 small corn tortillas, 6 inches in diameter
1 cup yogurt or sour cream, for garnish
1 cup guacamole, for garnish (optional)
3 radishes, thinly sliced, for garnish

In a blender or food processor, blend together the tomatillos, yogurt, cottage cheese, and cilantro until smooth. Set aside.

In a small microwavable dish, combine the oil and onion. Microwave on HIGH for 2 to 3 minutes, or until the onion is tender. Cool slightly. Stir in the chilies and 1½ cups of the cheese.

Wrap tortillas in a double layer of paper towels. Microwave on HIGH for 1 minute, or just until warm and softened. Be careful not to overheat: They will become dry and brittle.

Place the tortillas, one at a time, on a flat surface. Sprinkle 2 heaping tablespoons of the cheese mixture on each tortilla. Roll tightly and place, seam side down, in two 9-inch square microwavable baking dishes. (In two dishes, the enchiladas seem to cook more evenly than in a 11 × 7-inch dish.) Pour sauce over the enchiladas and sprinkle with the remaining cheese. Cover loosely with plastic wrap. Microwave on MEDIUM for 4 to 6 minutes, or until heated through, rotating the dish after 2 minutes. Let stand, covered, for 3 minutes.

To serve, place 2 enchiladas on a plate and top with a dollop of yogurt. Place a mound of guacamole on top, if desired. Garnish with radish slices.

Makes 8 enchiladas, 4 servings as a main course

N O T E : Lime-treated corn tortillas provide high levels of calcium that can be utilized by the body in much the same way as dairy products. Check package labels.

AS AN ASIDE

Herbed Green and Yellow Squash
Cinnamon-scented Kabocha Squash
Squash and Apple Bake
Broccoli and Red Pepper Medley
Beet and Parsnip Puree
Herbed Corn on the Cob
Indian Cauliflower and Peas
Okra and Tomatoes
Mushrooms and Leeks
Hot Greens and Corn
Spicy Brussels Sprouts
Snow Peas and Carrots
Fresh Peas and Lettuce
Silver Queen Succotash
Dilled Green Bean and Red Radish Salad
White Bean Salad with Sage and Fresh Mint
Key Lime Speckled Butter Beans
Tres Frijoles with Gremolata Dressing
Minted Quinoa Salad
Green Bean and Orange Rice Salad
Apple Curry Rice
Greek Spinach Rice
Basmati Rice Pilaf
Multigrain Pilaf
R. J.'s Roasted Potatoes
Yam Salad

Vegetarian foods are as colorful as they are delicious. One of the joys of cooking vegetable side dishes in the microwave is that the colors are absolutely vibrant. Because microwave cooking uses such a small amount of water, natural colors are enhanced. Nutrients are retained to a greater degree than in conventional cooking. So expect vegetables that are more beautiful and flavorful than ever before.

Not all of the side dishes here are vegetables. You'll find some nice grain and bean accompaniments too. If you are into mixing and matching, the wide assortment of recipes will let you serve several together that will make a terrific meal. You may find that combining two or three side dishes can make an interesting and colorful presentation.

In many cases adding some tofu, cheese, and nuts will round out the protein of the side dish to give you a well-balanced menu.

HERBED GREEN AND YELLOW SQUASH

This simple combination couldn't be easier to prepare. You can prepare it several hours or a day in advance and serve it at room temperature or slightly chilled. I like to use a Wisconsin Asiago cheese here as a nice alternative to Parmesan cheese.

1 tablespoon olive oil
1 garlic clove, minced
2 medium green and yellow summer squash, (1 green and 1 yellow),
   cut into ¼-inch slices (about 2 pounds)
1 teaspoon chopped basil or ½ teaspoon dried basil
1 teaspoon chopped thyme or ½ teaspoon dried thyme
¼ teaspoon dried rosemary
1 scallion, white part only, thinly sliced
1 medium tomato, diced
¼ teaspoon freshly ground white pepper
2 tablespoons grated Asiago cheese

Combine the oil and garlic in a 2-quart microwavable casserole. Microwave on HIGH for 30 seconds. Add the squash, basil, thyme, and rosemary. Cover tightly with a lid or vented plastic wrap. Microwave on HIGH for 5 to 6 minutes, or until the squash is tender-crisp.

Stir in the scallion, tomato, and pepper. Re-cover and microwave on HIGH 1 minute longer. Let stand, covered, for 3 to 4 minutes. Sprinkle with grated cheese and serve.

Makes 4 to 6 servings

CINNAMON-SCENTED KABOCHA SQUASH

Kabocha squash is my all-time favorite winter squash, bar none. A Japanese variety, it has either a pale green-gray or orange shell and a flattened ball shape. It is a rich and sweetly flavored squash that needs little or no seasonings. Here it is merely steamed with some orange juice and cinnamon, though you could include some melted butter if you care to. Like all winter squashes, it is a good source of vitamins A and C, along with niacin, phosphorus, and potassium.

1 medium Kabocha squash (about 2½ pounds)
½ cup orange juice
1 teaspoon ground cinnamon
Salt

Pierce the squash in 3 or 4 places with the tip of a sharp knife. Place the squash on a double layer of paper towels on the floor of the oven. Microwave on HIGH for 8 minutes, turning once. Let stand until the squash is cool enough to handle, about 10 minutes.

Cut the squash in half and scoop out the seeds. Cut the halves into chunks about 2 × 1 inches. Arrange the squash on a 12-inch glass plate, placing the lesser cooked pieces around the outside of the plate. Place the orange juice and cinnamon in a small bowl; stir well to combine. Pour over the squash. Cover loosely with vented plastic wrap. Microwave on HIGH for 5 to 7 minutes, or until the squash is tender. Let stand, covered, for 3 minutes.

Sprinkle lightly with salt and serve, making sure to spoon up some of the sauce from the bottom of the platter.

Makes 4 servings

SQUASH AND APPLE BAKE

Thanks to Frieda of California, more than twelve varieties of hard-shelled squash are available in the markets with new ones coming in each year. Sweet Dumpling, a small pumpkin-shaped squash with a streaked white and green shell, is an attractive addition to roster of the winter squashes. Golden Nugget, which is small and round, can also be used in this recipe. And if you can't find either, acorn squash will do just fine.

2 Sweet Dumpling or Golden Nugget squash (about 1¼ pounds each)
2 tablespoons vegetable oil
1 tablespoon lemon juice
1 large Granny Smith apple, cored and diced
1 medium leek, white part only, thinly sliced
½ teaspoon salt
¼ teaspoon ground cinnamon
¼ teaspoon ground nutmeg
⅛ teaspoon ground allspice
⅛ teaspoon ground white pepper

Pierce the squash in 3 or 4 places with the tip of a sharp knife. Place the squash on a double layer of paper towels on the floor of the oven. Microwave on HIGH for 4 minutes. Turn the squash and microwave on HIGH for 4 to 6 minutes longer, or until it just begins to feel soft when gently squeezed. Let stand until cooled, about 5 minutes.

Meanwhile, in a 2-quart oval casserole or 9-inch glass pie plate, combine the oil, lemon juice, apple, leek, salt, cinnamon, nutmeg, allspice, and pepper. Cover tightly with a lid or vented plastic wrap. Microwave on HIGH for 5 minutes, or until the apple and leek are quite soft.

Cut the squash in half and scoop out the seeds. Scoop the pulp from the squash into the casserole with the apple mixture. Mash the squash with the back of a spoon while stirring in the apple and leek to combine. Spoon the mixture back into the casserole or pie plate.

(continued)

(continued)

Cover loosely with a lid or vented plastic wrap. Microwave on HIGH for 4 to 6 minutes, or until heated through.

Makes 4 servings

BROCCOLI AND RED PEPPER MEDLEY

This low-fat way to prepare broccoli is a real winner. Red pepper gives a bright contrast and the leeks lend a nice touch. There are good sources of vitamins A and C here along with dietary fiber. Color, flavor, and texture all add up to a winning combination.

1 head broccoli (about 1½ pounds)
2 tablespoons water
1 tablespoon olive oil
1 small red bell pepper, seeded and diced
⅓ cup thinly sliced leek, white part only
½ teaspoon dried thyme
2 tablespoons grated Parmesan cheese

Wash and trim the broccoli. Use the florets and about 1 inch of the stems. Cut the florets into 1-inch pieces, and the stems into ½-inch slices. In a 10-inch round microwavable baking dish or glass pie plate, arrange the florets in the center with the stems around the outside. Sprinkle with 2 tablespoons water. Cover tightly with vented plastic wrap and microwave on HIGH for 5 minutes, or until very crisp. Let stand, covered for 3 minutes.

Uncover and drizzle with oil. Sprinkle the pepper, leeks, and thyme over the top. Re-cover with vented plastic wrap and microwave on HIGH for 1 minute. Let stand, covered, for 3 minutes. Sprinkle with cheese and serve.

Makes 4 servings

BEET AND PARSNIP PUREE

Beets are so brilliant in color that even when they are blended with parsnips, they make this side dish a real eye-catcher.

3 large beets, with stems trimmed to 1 inch and roots intact, scrubbed,
    (about 5 ounces each)
½ cup water, divided
1 large parsnip, peeled and chopped
½ cup chopped onion
¾ teaspoon chopped ginger
¼ teaspoon ground nutmeg
¼ cup sour cream or yogurt
½ teaspoon salt
Freshly ground black pepper to taste

Place the beets in a 1-quart microwavable casserole and add ¼ cup of the water. Cover tightly with a lid or vented plastic wrap. Microwave on HIGH for 12 to 16 minutes, or until the beets are tender, stirring after 6 minutes. Let stand, covered, for 5 minutes. Place beets in a bowl of cold water to cool slightly. Slip off the skins and cut into 1-inch chunks.

In a 1-quart microwavable casserole, combine the remaining water, the parsnip, onion, ginger, and nutmeg. Cover tightly with a lid or vented plastic wrap. Microwave on HIGH for 4 to 6 minutes, or until the parsnip is tender. Let stand, covered, for 5 minutes. Drain.

Puree the beets, parsnip, and onion in a food processor. Add the sour cream or yogurt and salt; process until smooth. Spoon into a serving dish. Add pepper to taste.

Makes 4 servings

HERBED CORN ON THE COB

Placing food in oven cooking bags evens out heat distribution and blends food flavors with herbs, not to mention eliminating cleanups from splatters. What this technique does for fresh corn is splendid.

1 tablespoon flour
2 tablespoons grated Parmesan cheese
½ teaspoon dried rosemary leaves, crushed
⅛ teaspoon freshly ground black pepper
¼ cup water
3 tablespoons butter or margarine, diced
4 medium ears fresh corn, husked

Place a large size (20 × 14 inches) cooking bag in a 13 × 8 × 2-inch microwavable baking dish, or a 12-inch round glass plate. Place the flour, cheese, rosemary, and pepper in the bag and shake to mix. Add the water and butter and squeeze the bag gently to blend. Place the corn in the bag in a single layer. Close the bag with a nylon tie, and make 6 half-inch slits in the top of bag. Microwave on HIGH for 5 minutes. Grasp the corners of the bag and shake gently to move each end piece to the center of the bag so that the middle ears are now on the outside. Microwave on HIGH for 5 minutes longer. Let stand for 3 minutes. To serve, slit the bag down the center, remove corn to a platter, and stir and spoon the herbed butter over the corn.

Makes 4 servings

INDIAN CAULIFLOWER AND PEAS

Each time you make this spicy dish it can be a new experience. Toss in some shredded unsweetened coconut in the first stage, or as a finishing touch. Add sesame seeds or roasted peanuts for a fuller flavor. In India, vegetables are not prepared to retain crispness as ours are, so you may want to add a few minutes to the cooking time for a more authentic version.

1 medium head cauliflower (about 1¼ pounds)
2 tablespoons peanut or vegetable oil
2 garlic cloves, minced
½ teaspoon mustard seeds
½ teaspoon ground turmeric
½ teaspoon ground cumin
¼ teaspoon ground coriander
¼ teaspoon ground red pepper
¼ cup water
1 cup fresh peas or frozen peas, defrosted
2 teaspoons lemon juice
Salt to taste

Break the cauliflower into florets and set aside. In a 3-quart microwavable casserole or oval baking dish, combine the oil and garlic. Microwave on HIGH for 1 minute. Stir in the mustard seeds, turmeric, cumin, coriander, and pepper. Microwave on HIGH for 2 to 3 minutes longer, or until the mustard seeds start to pop.

Add the cauliflower to the casserole in batches, stirring well to coat with oil and spices, and pour in the water. Cover tightly with a lid or vented plastic wrap and microwave on HIGH for 8 to 10 minutes, or until the cauliflower is tender. Stir in the peas. Re-cover and microwave on HIGH for 1 minute. Let stand, covered, for 5 minutes. Stir in the lemon juice and salt to taste and serve.

Makes 4 servings

OKRA AND TOMATOES

Since brass, copper, or iron are never used in a microwave oven, you won't have to worry about okra that is grayish or has a tinny taste. Choose smaller, brightly colored pods and snip off just a tip of the stem. This savory stew becomes a main dish when you add corn and chick peas or diced tofu. On its own, it's a good source of calcium, iron, and vitamin C.

3 tablespoons olive oil
2 garlic cloves, minced
1 pound okra, washed and trimmed
1 pound tomatoes, cored and coarsely chopped
1 teaspoon dried basil
½ teaspoon dried thyme
½ teaspoon dried marjoram
½ teaspoon crushed red pepper
Freshly ground black pepper to taste

In a 3-quart microwavable casserole, combine the oil and garlic. Microwave on HIGH for 1 minute. Stir in the okra, tossing well to coat. Microwave on HIGH for 5 minutes, stirring once. Add the tomatoes, basil, thyme, marjoram, and red pepper. Cover tightly with a lid or vented plastic wrap. Microwave on HIGH for 4 to 7 minutes, or until the okra is tender and the tomatoes are softened, stirring once. Let stand, covered, for 5 minutes. Add freshly ground black pepper to taste.

Makes 4 to 6 servings

MUSHROOMS AND LEEKS

Straight from the fourteenth-century court of Richard II, who was called "the best and royalest viander of all Christian Kings," comes this easy and sublime combination. Taken from the book *To the King's Taste*, this dish, says author Lorna J. Sass, "is a culinary marriage made in heaven." I think you'll agree. It's a lovely accompaniment to rice or beans as well as on its own.

5 small leeks, white parts with ½ inch of green parts, trimmed
6 tablespoons butter, divided
1 pound large mushrooms, trimmed and quartered
1 cup Basic Vegetable Stock (page 199)
½ teaspoon brown sugar
½ teaspoon minced ginger
⅛ teaspoon saffron
3 tablespoons unbleached white flour
¼ teaspoon salt
¼ teaspoon freshly ground black pepper

Wash leeks thoroughly, making sure to remove as much sand and grit as possible. Cut into ¼-inch slices and set aside.

Place 3 tablespoons of the butter in a 3-quart microwavable casserole. Microwave on HIGH for 1 minute, or until the butter is melted. Add the leeks and toss with the butter until coated. Microwave on HIGH for 3 minutes, or until the leeks are wilted, stirring once.

Add the mushrooms and stir until coated with butter. Stir in the stock, sugar, ginger, and saffron. Cover tightly with a lid or vented plastic wrap. Microwave on HIGH for 2 to 4 minutes, or until just boiling.

In a small bowl, combine the remaining butter, the flour, salt, and pepper to form a smooth paste. Add the flour mixture to the leeks and mushrooms, stirring until thoroughly blended. Microwave on HIGH, uncovered, for 3 to 5 minutes, or until boiling and slightly thickened.

Makes 4 servings

HOT GREENS AND CORN

Kale and collards, loaded with vitamins and minerals, are important sources of nutrients for vegetarians. The greens are often prepared with lots of fat. This flavorful version was developed by Mike Center, a health-minded friend, with but a whisper of oil.

2 pounds kale or collards
2 tablespoons vegetable oil
2 garlic cloves, minced
1 medium leek, white part only, thoroughly washed and coarsely chopped
½ cup Basic Vegetable Stock (page 199) or water
1 tablespoon rice vinegar
½ teaspoon crushed red pepper
¼ teaspoon salt
1 ear corn, cooked and kernels removed or 1 cup drained canned corn
¼ cup rice vinegar
2 small tomatoes, quartered, for garnish

Rinse greens under cold running water. Strip the leaves from the thick bottom stems, keeping the tender top stem and leaf attached. (Discard the bottom portion or reserve for stock.) Gather the leaves, stack them, and slice into ¼-inch strips. Set aside.

In a 5-quart microwavable casserole, combine the vegetable oil, garlic, and leek. Microwave on HIGH for 2 minutes. Add the greens, stock, vinegar, pepper, and salt, tossing until combined. Cover with a lid or vented plastic wrap. Microwave on HIGH for 5 to 7 minutes, or until the greens are wilted, stirring once during cooking.

Stir in the corn (and additional liquid if the casserole is very dry). Re-cover and microwave on HIGH for 3 to 6 minutes, or until the greens are tender. Stir in the rice vinegar. Re-cover and let stand for 3 minutes.

Transfer the greens to a large platter and garnish with the tomatoes.

Makes 4 to 6 servings

SPICY BRUSSELS SPROUTS

Mike Center, my good friend, and a wonderful cook, developed this recipe for everyone who absolutely hates Brussels sprouts. The contrast of the lime juice and the jalapeño jelly may turn this into a favorite vegetable for lots of folks.

1 pound Brussels sprouts
2 tablespoons water
2 tablespoons vegetable oil or butter
Juice of 1 small lime
¼ teaspoon salt
2 tablespoons jalapeño jelly

Cut off the root ends of the Brussels sprouts and remove loose outer leaves. Slice the sprouts lengthwise into ¼- or ⅛-inch sections.

In a shallow 2-quart microwavable casserole or baking dish, combine the sprouts, water, oil, lime juice, and salt. Cover tightly with a lid or vented plastic wrap. Microwave on HIGH for 3 minutes, then stir. Re-cover and microwave on HIGH for 2 to 5 minutes, or until the sprouts are tender-crisp. Stir in the jalapeño jelly and serve.

Makes 4 servings

SNOW PEAS AND CARROTS

Turn everyday peas and carrots into a welcome new side dish. Snow peas really brighten it up, making it festive enough for a holiday meal. Fresh dill makes a lively addition.

1 medium onion, thinly sliced
2 tablespoons Clarified Butter (page 208) or olive oil
2 medium carrots, peeled and cut into 2 x ¼-inch strips
½ pound snow peas, trimmed
3 tablespoons chopped dill or 2 teaspoons dried dillweed
Salt and freshly ground black pepper to taste

In a 2-quart microwavable casserole or oval dish, combine the onion and butter, stirring well to coat. Microwave on HIGH for 1 minute. Stir in the carrots; cover tightly with a lid or vented plastic wrap. Microwave on HIGH for 2 minutes. Stir in the snow peas and dill. Re-cover and microwave on HIGH for 6 to 8 minutes, or until the vegetables are tender-crisp. Let stand, covered, for 3 minutes. Add salt and pepper to taste.

Makes 4 servings

FRESH PEAS AND LETTUCE

This classic French side dish is a beauty and wonderfully simple to make. I prefer it with just a sprinkle of salt and pepper, but you can toss in some mint or thyme if you like.

2 tablespoons butter
2 cups fresh peas or frozen tiny peas, defrosted (10-ounce package)
4 large Boston lettuce leaves, shredded

¼ teaspoon sugar (optional)
Salt and freshly ground black pepper to taste

Place the butter in a 2-quart microwavable casserole. Microwave on HIGH for 1 minute, or until the butter is melted. Stir in the peas, lettuce, and sugar, if desired. Cover tightly with a lid or vented plastic wrap. Microwave on HIGH for 6 to 8 minutes, or until the peas are tender and the lettuce is wilted. Let stand, covered, for 3 minutes. Add salt and pepper to taste.

Makes 4 servings

SILVER QUEEN SUCCOTASH

White Silver Queen corn is incredibly flavorful, and it is stunning with lima beans and red pepper. Use a strong extra-virgin olive oil or an unrefined corn oil for full flavor. Add some summer savory if you like, but I think a sprinkle of salt and fresh pepper does just fine.

2 tablespoons olive or corn oil
2 ears white corn (about 2 cups), kernels removed
2 cups cooked lima beans or frozen baby lima beans, defrosted (10-ounce package)
1 small red bell pepper, seeded and diced
¼ teaspoon salt
¼ teaspoon freshly ground black pepper

In a 3-quart microwavable casserole, combine the oil, corn, lima beans, and pepper, tossing well to coat with oil. Cover tightly with a lid or vented plastic wrap. Microwave on HIGH for 5 to 8 minutes, or until heated through and the corn is crisp.

Stir in the salt and pepper. Let stand, covered, for 3 minutes.

Makes 4 servings

DILLED GREEN BEAN AND
RED RADISH SALAD

Whole green beans topped with finely chopped red radishes are a bright combination. For an equally pretty plate, I sometimes toss the beans with cooked julienned carrots instead of the radishes. If you like a creamier dressing than the vinaigrette suggested here, try the Yogurt-Cucumber Dressing (page 211).

1 pound green beans, washed and trimmed
¼ cup water
2 tablespoons white wine vinegar
1 tablespoon lemon juice
1 tablespoon chopped dill or 1 teaspoon dried dillweed
1 teaspoon dry mustard
1 teaspoon salt
¼ teaspoon freshly ground black pepper
⅓ cup canola oil
2 tablespoons walnut oil
2 red radishes, finely chopped, for garnish

Place the beans in a 1½-quart microwavable casserole and add the water. Cover tightly with vented plastic wrap and microwave on HIGH for 8 to 12 minutes, or until the beans are tender-crisp. Let stand, covered, for 5 minutes.

Meanwhile, in a small bowl, combine the vinegar, lemon juice, dill, mustard, salt, and pepper. Slowly whisk in the canola and walnut oils in a steady stream. Uncover the beans and blanch under cold water to maintain color, if desired. Drain well. Arrange the beans on a serving platter, cover, and refrigerate.

Just before serving, pour about half of the dressing over the beans, or to taste, reserving the remainder for another use. Sprinkle with the chopped radishes.

Makes 4 servings

WHITE BEAN SALAD WITH SAGE AND FRESH MINT

Sometimes the simplest dishes are the most enjoyable. This chilled side dish gets extra flavor from a clove-studded onion and carrot that are added to the bean cooking water. Add a light dressing laced with sage leaves and fresh mint, *et voila!*, a pleasant French salad.

2 cups dried beans, such as navy or Great Northern beans
1 small onion, cut in half
4 cloves
1 medium carrot, washed and cut in thirds
3 tablespoons white wine vinegar
3 tablespoons Dijon mustard
⅓ cup olive oil
3 tablespoons chopped sage
3 tablespoons chopped mint
Salt and freshly ground black pepper to taste
Chopped parsley, for garnish (optional)

Rinse the beans in cold water. Prepare according to the directions on page 103. After presoaking the beans, pierce the onion halves with the cloves. Add the onion and carrot to the cooking water; proceed as directed, then remove the onion and carrot from the drained, cooked beans.

In a small bowl, combine the vinegar and mustard, then whisk in the oil. Pour over the beans. Add the sage, mint, salt, and pepper to taste and toss well. Cover and refrigerate for at least 3 hours. Stir again before serving. Adjust the seasonings if necessary and garnish with chopped parsley, if desired.

Makes 8 servings

KEY LIME SPECKLED BUTTER BEANS

I was cooking some dried Dixie Speckled Butter beans from Dean & Deluca, a gourmet shop in New York City, for the first time without a thought as to how I would serve them. Leftover Key Lime juice sparked the inspiration and the rest just fell into place. The salad stands well on its own or blends deliciously with leftover grains for a light entree.

1 cup dried Dixie Speckled Butter beans or red kidney beans, cooked (page 251)
⅓ cup chopped red onion
¼ cup Key Lime juice or fresh lime juice
3 tablespoons olive oil
3 tablespoons chopped parsley
1 teaspoon dried thyme, crumbled
1 teaspoon salt
¼ teaspoon crushed red pepper

In a medium mixing bowl, combine all the ingredients, stirring well to blend. Cover and refrigerate for at least 3 hours. Stir again before serving. Adjust the seasonings if necessary.

Makes 4 servings

TRES FRIJOLES WITH GREMOLATA DRESSING

I was testing some Italian recipes when I first discovered gremolata, a simple mixture of garlic, lemon peel, and parsley traditionally served with osso bucco, an Italian veal dish. I thought at the time that this could make a nice addition to a beans. Later I stumbled on Tres Frijoles, a mixture of dried red kidney and black turtle beans and chick peas, packaged by Dean & Deluca, a gourmet food store in New York City. The gremolata, along with some olive oil and balsamic vinegar, is a superb companion for these beans. Prepare this dish a day or two ahead for best flavor.

¼ cup olive oil
2 garlic cloves, minced
⅓ cup chopped Italian parsley
Peel of 1 lemon, yellow part only, finely chopped
¼ cup finely chopped red onion
3 tablespoons balsamic vinegar
2 tablespoons lemon juice
½ teaspoon salt
¼ teaspoon freshly ground black pepper
3 cups cooked Tres Frijoles or mixed beans (page 251)

In a 1-cup glass measure, combine the oil and garlic. Microwave on HIGH for 1 minute. Add the parsley and lemon peel. Microwave on HIGH for 1 minute. Stir and let cool for several minutes. Stir in the onion, vinegar, lemon juice, salt, and pepper. Pour the dressing over the beans and toss well to combine.

Cover and refrigerate for several hours or overnight. Serve at room temperature.

Makes 4 servings

MINTED QUINOA SALAD

Fresh mint makes this grain dish a deliciously refreshing accompaniment at lunch or dinner. Serve just slightly chilled or at room temperature. Pronounced keen-wa, this South American grain contains complete protein of an unusually high quality. It also has a slightly nutty flavor. Look for it in health-food stores or in gourmet supermarkets.

2 cups Basic Vegetable Stock (page 199)
1 cup quinoa
½ teaspoon salt
1 garlic clove, minced
1 carrot, finely grated
⅓ cup dark raisins
3 tablespoons chopped mint
3 tablespoons olive oil
3 tablespoons balsamic vinegar
2 tablespoons fresh lemon juice
¼ teaspoon ground red pepper

In a 1½-quart microwavable dish, combine the stock, quinoa, and salt. Cover tightly with a lid or vented plastic wrap. Microwave on HIGH for 5 minutes, or until boiling, then microwave on MEDIUM for 10 minutes longer, or until most of the stock is absorbed. Let stand, covered, for 5 minutes. (Any remaining stock will be absorbed on standing.)

Remove the cover and fluff with a fork. Add the garlic, carrot, raisins, mint, oil, vinegar, lemon juice, and pepper, mixing well to combine. Cover and refrigerate for at least 1 hour. Serve at room temperature.

Makes 4 to 6 servings

GREEN BEAN AND ORANGE RICE SALAD

When you're looking for a light and colorful side dish, this is one to try. The rice takes on an especially nice flavor when orange juice is added to the cooking water. But if you already have some plain cooked rice on hand, go ahead and use it.

1 pound green beans, trimmed and cut on the diagonal into 1½-inch pieces
2 tablespoons water
2 tablespoons vegetable oil
2 garlic cloves, minced
2 oranges
1 cup plain yogurt
1 tablespoon chopped tarragon or 1 teaspoon dried tarragon, crumbled
3 cups cooked brown rice (cooked in ¾ cup orange juice and 1¾ cups water, if desired)
½ cup chopped celery
2 scallions, white and green parts kept separate, thinly sliced
Salt and freshly ground black pepper to taste

Place the green beans in a 2-quart microwavable casserole and sprinkle with water. Cover with vented plastic wrap and microwave on HIGH for 7 to 10 minutes, or until tender, stirring once. Let stand, covered, for 3 minutes. Uncover, drain off any excess water and set aside.

Place oil and garlic in a small microwavable bowl. Microwave on HIGH for 1 minute. Grate the peel, orange part only, and squeeze the juice from 1 orange; add both to the oil and garlic. Stir in the yogurt and tarragon until blended. Peel and section the remaining orange by carefully cutting just deep enough to remove the white pith.

In a large serving bowl, combine the green beans, orange sections, rice, celery, and white parts of the scallions. Pour the dressing over the top and toss well to combine. Sprinkle the green parts of the scallions over the salad for garnish.

Makes 6 servings

APPLE CURRY RICE

The subtle taste of curry and the tart apple contrast to make this side dish something special. It serves well hot or at room temperature. Don't be afraid of leftovers here, because the addition of chopped celery and tofu turn them into an easy luncheon dish.

½ cup water
½ cup raisins
2 tablespoons vegetable oil
½ cup chopped onion
2 teaspoons curry powder
½ teaspoon freshly ground black pepper
1 Golden Delicious apple, peeled, cored, and chopped
3 cups cooked brown rice (cooked in ¾ cup apple juice and 1¾ cups water, if desired)
Salt to taste

Pour the water into a 2-cup glass measure and microwave on HIGH for 1 minute. Add the raisins and soak for 5 minutes. Drain, and set aside. Place the oil, onion, curry powder, and pepper in a 2-quart microwavable casserole and stir to combine. Microwave on HIGH for 2 minutes, or until the onions are tender.

Add the apple, tossing well to coat; stir in the rice. Re-cover and cook on HIGH for 3 to 5 minutes, or until rice is heated through. Add the raisins. Re-cover and let stand for 2 minutes. Add salt to taste, if desired, and serve.

Makes 4 to 6 servings

GREEK SPINACH RICE

This side dish has long been a favorite of mine. In restaurants, it's always made with white rice; I must admit that the nutty taste and texture of brown rice makes it even better.

2 tablespoons olive oil
2 garlic cloves, minced
½ cup thinly sliced scallions, including 1-inch of the green parts
1 cup white or brown rice
8 ounces spinach, washed, trimmed, and shredded (about 3 heaping cups)
2 cups Mushroom Stock (page 201)
1 teaspoon grated lemon peel
½ teaspoon freshly ground white pepper
¼ teaspoon grated nutmeg

In a 3-quart microwavable casserole, combine the oil, garlic, and scallions. Microwave on HIGH for 1 minute. Add the rice and stir until well coated. Microwave on HIGH for 2 minutes. Stir in the spinach and stock. Cover tightly with a lid or vented plastic wrap. Microwave on HIGH for 4 to 6 minutes, until boiling.

Reduce setting to MEDIUM and cook for 30 to 40 minutes (depending on whether you are using white or brown rice), or until almost all of the liquid is absorbed. Stir in the lemon peel, pepper, and nutmeg. Re-cover and let stand for 5 minutes.

Makes 4 servings

BASMATI RICE PILAF

Basmati rice is a highly aromatic grain with a slightly sweet flavor. A staple in Indian cooking, it's widely available in health-food stores and Indian specialty shops. This recipe uses the brown basmati which retains a layer of bran and has a somewhat nutty taste. Add some cashews and chopped dried apricots for a fancier dish.

1 cup finely chopped onion
1 tablespoon canola oil
½ teaspoon cumin seeds
1 cup brown basmati rice
2½ cups water or Basic Vegetable Stock (page 199)
1 cinnamond stick (about 3 inches)
2 tablespoons chopped parsley
Salt and freshly ground black pepper to taste

In a 3-quart microwavable casserole, combine the onion, oil, and cumin seeds. Microwave on HIGH for 2 minutes. Add the rice and stir until the grains are coated. Microwave on HIGH for 2 minutes. Add the water and cinnamon stick. Cover tightly with a lid or vented plastic wrap. Microwave on HIGH for 6 to 8 minutes, or until boiling. Reduce setting to MEDIUM and cook for 40 to 45 minutes, or until the liquid is absorbed. Let stand, covered, for 5 minutes. Stir in the parsley and add salt and pepper to taste.

Makes 4 to 6 servings

MULTIGRAIN PILAF

This easy side dish is a perfect accompaniment to most any meal. Use it as a base for a warm or chilled salad, tossing it with tofu, nuts, and leftover vegetables. It's great as part of a stuffing and the pilaf used in Stuffed Acorn Squash (page 131).

2 tablespoons canola oil
½ cup thinly sliced scallions, including green parts
1 medium carrot, peeled and coarsely chopped
1 cup Multigrain Mix (page 229)
2⅔ cups Basic Vegetable Stock (page 199) or water
¼ cup chopped parsley
Salt and freshly ground black pepper to taste

In a 3-quart microwavable casserole, combine the oil and scallions. Microwave on HIGH for 1 minute. Stir in the carrot and grain mix, coating the grains with oil. Microwave on HIGH for 2 minutes. Stir in the stock and parsley. Cover tightly with a lid or vented plastic wrap. Microwave on HIGH for 6 to 8 minutes, or until boiling. Reduce setting to MEDIUM and cook for 40 to 45 minutes, or until the grains are tender and almost all of the liquid is absorbed. (Add additional stock if necessary.) Let stand, covered, for 5 minutes. Fluff with a fork, add salt and pepper to taste and serve.

Makes 4 servings

R.J.'S ROASTED POTATOES

This may be one of the simplest and tastiest recipes in the book. My sister, R. J. (for Rita-Jane), likes to roast potatoes in the oven for a side dish that everyone enjoys. She has since discovered that the microwave makes it faster than ever.

10 small new potatoes, scrubbed (about 2 pounds)
16 large garlic cloves, peeled
2 tablespoons olive oil
½ teaspoon salt
½ teaspoon freshly ground black pepper

Pierce the potatoes with a fork. Peel a ½-inch strip of the skin from around the middle of each potato. Place the potatoes and garlic cloves in a 10-inch glass pie plate or shallow baking dish. Drizzle with oil and sprinkle salt and pepper over the top. Stir to coat the garlic and potatoes completely with oil. Microwave on HIGH for 6 to 9 minutes, or until the potatoes are tender when pierced with the tip of a small knife, stirring once during cooking to rearrange the potatoes. Let stand for 5 minutes. Stir again to coat and serve.

Makes 3 to 4 servings

YAM SALAD

While sweet potatoes and yams are actually two different plants, it's the true yam that is sweeter and moister and that you'll want to use in this recipe whenever possible. Sweet potatoes can be substituted if necessary. Choose firm, smooth-skinned sweets of medium size.

6 yams, scrubbed (about 8 ounces each)
¾ cup plain yogurt
¼ cup mayonnaise
2 tablespoons lemon juice
2 tablespoons chopped chives or 1 tablespoon dried chives
1 tablespoon curry powder
½ cup finely chopped red onion
½ cup finely chopped celery
Salt and freshly ground black pepper to taste
Red leaf lettuce
Chopped cilantro, for garnish

Pierce the yams with a fork. Place on a double layer of paper towels in a circle on the floor of the oven, leaving about 1 inch between each one. Microwave on HIGH for 10 to 14 minutes, or until tender, turning once during cooking. Let stand for 5 to 10 minutes, with each wrapped in a paper towel. Cool, then peel and cut the yams into 1-inch cubes.

In a medium bowl, whisk together the yogurt, mayonnaise, lemon juice, chives, and curry powder. In a large bowl, combine the yams, onion, and celery. Pour the dressing over the yams and toss lightly to combine. Add salt and pepper to taste. Arrange lettuce leaves on individual plates or on a large serving platter and mound the salad on top. Sprinkle with cilantro just before serving.

Makes 6 to 8 servings

NOTE: If preparing the salad the night before, reserve about a third of the dressing. Bring the salad to room temperature and stir in the remainder of the dressing.

SWEETS AND TREATS

Fresh Fruit Compote
Poached Pears with Red Wine and Cassis
Baked Apples or Pears
Applesauce
Banana Bundt Cake
Sweet Potato–Apple Cake
Cocoa Brownies
Rhubarb-Pear Crisp
Peach Pandowdy
Pie Crusts
Cranberry Linzer Tart
Summer Fruit Tart
Pumpkin Cheesecake Pie
Pumpkin-Tofu Pie
Lombardy Custard
Molasses Corn Pudding
Steamed Date Pudding
Amasake Pudding
Rich Rice Pudding
Rice Pudding
Golden Apple Bread Pudding
Stephen's Bread Pudding

If you've never considered yourself a dessert maker, just wait until you try some of the recipes here. You will please yourself, and impress your guests, with the delicious desserts you make in a flash.

It seems as though the microwave was made just for preparing many of the traditional desserts. Creamy rice puddings, dried fruit compotes, and crumbly fruit crisps couldn't be easier than they are here.

Seasonal fresh fruits poached in simple syrups or in elegant wine combinations and creamy cheesecakes are perfect candidates for microwave preparation. Though many cakes are not always at their best when done in the microwave, I think you'll find the Banana Bundt and the Sweet Potato–Apple Cake very pleasing renditions.

Lack of time will no longer be a factor to restrict your making desserts. Many fruits, for instance, can be left unpeeled and sometimes a recipe requires little more than a spoon, a suitable dish, and a microwave oven.

FRESH FRUIT COMPOTE

I like to mix different kinds of pears and apples when making this. Whatever is waiting at the market offers a nice variation in both flavor and texture. Leaving the peel on the fruits also provides added character. Toss in some toasted walnuts at the end for a nutty crunch.

1 pound apples, cored and cut into ½-inch pieces (about 3 medium)
1 pound pears, cored and cut into ½-inch pieces (about 2 medium)
1 cup dark raisins
½ cup orange juice
2 tablespoons packed brown sugar
1 tablespoon lemon juice
2 slices fresh ginger, about ½ inch thick
¼ teaspoon ground allspice
½ cup chopped walnuts, toasted (page 24)

In a 2-quart microwavable casserole, combine the apples, pears, raisins, orange juice, sugar, lemon juice, ginger, and allspice. Cover tightly with a lid or vented plastic wrap. Microwave on HIGH for 9 to 14 minutes, or until the fruits have softened, stirring after 5 minutes. Stir in the nuts. Re-cover and let stand for 15 minutes. Remove the ginger slices. Serve warm.

Makes 4 servings

POACHED PEARS WITH RED WINE AND CASSIS

Pears are especially pretty when poached in red wine. Cassis gives them a richer flavor. Use this recipe as a basic one and experiment with a variety of other poaching liquids (white wine, orange or cranberry juice). The cooking liquid can be saved and used to prepare other fruits. It also reduces to a beautiful, shiny syrup that, together with a few leaves of fresh mint, makes for a great dessert.

4 firm, ripe Bosc or Comice pears, (about 8 ounces each)
3 cups cold water
2 tablespoons lemon juice
2 cups red wine
¾ cup sugar
⅓ cup Crème de Cassis
1 strip lemon peel, yellow part only, (2 x ½ inch)
1 Fresh mint, for garnish (optional)

Peel and core the pears, leaving the stems intact. Cut off the base of the pears so that they can be placed upright on the dessert plate when serving. Place in large bowl of water with lemon juice to prevent discoloration.

In a deep 3-quart microwavable casserole, combine the wine, sugar, cassis, and lemon peel. Microwave on HIGH, uncovered, for 3 minutes, or until just boiling. Stir until the sugar is completely dissolved.

Drain the pears and place in the casserole with the wine mixture; add just enough water (about 3 cups) to cover the pears. Cover tightly with a lid or vented plastic wrap. Microwave on HIGH for 5 to 7 minutes, or until the pears are easily pierced with the tip of a sharp knife. Rotate the dish once during cooking. Let the pears cool, uncovered, in the poaching liquid, turning occasionally so that they color evenly. Cover and refrigerate until ready to serve. The pears can be served slightly chilled or at room temperature. Prepare syrup (see Note), if desired.

Remove the pears with a slotted spoon to drain off any excess liquid. Stand upright on dessert plates or in small shallow dishes. Drizzle with the reduced poaching syrup (see Note) and garnish with mint leaves, if desired.

Makes 4 servings

N O T E : To make the syrup, microwave the remaining poaching liquid on HIGH, uncovered, for 20 to 30 minutes or until it is thick and syrupy. You should have about 1 cup. Rotate the dish at 10 minute intervals, stirring several times at each turn.

BAKED APPLES OR PEARS

This is a quick snack or dessert. The ingredients here are enough for one serving; the timing for up to four pieces of fruit is given in the note at the end of the recipe. Remember that small, juicy apples and pears cook faster than larger, drier ones.

• •

1 large whole apple or pear
1 tablespoon packed brown sugar
1 cinnamon stick (about 2 inches) or ⅛ teaspoon ground cinnamon
1 teaspoon butter or margarine
2 tablespoons water

• •

Core the apple or pear and pierce the skin around the center to prevent bursting. Place in a small microwavable dish (or casserole if more than one is being cooked). Fill the fruit with the brown sugar, cinnamon, and butter. Spoon water around the sides of the fruit. Cover loosely with vented plastic wrap. Microwave on HIGH for 2 to 4 minutes, or until the fruit is tender. Adjust the time for the additional number of fruits cooked.

Makes 1 serving

N O T E : For 2 pieces of fruit, allow 4 to 6 minutes; for 3, 6 to 8 minutes; for 4, 9 to 12 minutes.

• •

APPLESAUCE

Leaving the skins on the apples during cooking intensifies the fresh fruit flavor. It also adds a slight rosy tint to the sauce. If you don't have a food mill, peel the apples first, then puree them in a food processor or press with a potato masher after cooking. I've yet to need any additional sweetener, but add some if you like.

. . . .

2 pounds cooking apples, cored and quartered (about 5 medium)
½ cup water
1 tablespoon lemon juice
3 whole cloves
3 allspice berries or ¼ teaspoon ground allspice
Brown sugar or honey to taste (optional)

. . . .

In a 2-quart microwavable casserole, combine the apples, water, lemon juice, cloves, and allspice. Cover tightly with a lid or vented plastic wrap. Microwave on HIGH for 10 to 12 minutes, or until the apples are tender when pierced with a fork, stirring once during cooking. Let stand, covered, for 5 minutes. Cool slightly. Remove the cloves and allspice berries. Put the apples, with their juices, through a food mill to puree. Pour into a bowl; stir in brown sugar or honey if desired.

Makes 3 cups

BANANA BUNDT CAKE

This cake is a delight to prepare. Light and full of banana flavor, it looks particularly impressive since it takes its shape from the bundt pan. The cake is not overly sweet and the nuts add nice crunch. Any variety of maple syrup will do, but the dark maple syrup enhances the color. For an extra-easy version of this cake, mix it using a food processor. Either way, it's never a chore to fix.

. . . .

2 tablespoons graham cracker crumbs or finely chopped nuts.
1 cup whole wheat flour

. . . .

1½ cups unbleached white flour
1 teaspoon baking powder
1 teaspoon baking soda
1 teaspoon ground cinnamon
½ teaspoon ground nutmeg
¾ cup vegetable oil
¾ cup packed brown sugar
¼ cup dark maple syrup
2 eggs, at room temperature
1 cup yogurt or sour cream
1 tablespoon lemon juice
3 medium bananas, peeled and quartered, (about 4 ounces each)
½ cup walnuts, coarsely chopped

Grease a 10- to 12-cup microwavable bundt pan. Sprinkle with the crumbs or nuts, turning the pan to coat all the surfaces well and evenly.

In a large mixing bowl, sift together the flours, baking powder, baking soda, cinnamon, and nutmeg. In another large bowl, beat together the oil and sugar on medium speed until well blended. Add the maple syrup and eggs, mixing until thoroughly combined. Add the yogurt, lemon juice, and bananas. Mix on low speed until the bananas are mashed but some small chunks are still visible; scrape down the sides of the bowl once or twice while mixing. Add the walnuts and flour mixture and mix on low speed until all the ingredients are thoroughly combined. Spoon the batter into the prepared pan, smoothing with the back of a spoon.

Place the pan in the oven on an inverted microwavable cereal bowl or rack. Microwave on MEDIUM for 9 minutes. Rotate twice during the cooking. Microwave on HIGH for 5 to 8 minutes, or until a toothpick inserted in the center comes out clean. Rotate twice during cooking. Be careful not to overcook. (The cake should still be moist on top. When it is lightly touched with your finger, spots will come off and the cake underneath should be dry.)

Let the cake stand on a heat-resistant surface for 12 minutes, with a knife, loosen cake from side of pan. Place a serving plate over the pan and invert. Firmly tap the bottom of the pan, gently unmold, and let the cake cool completely. (Don't be concerned if the top of the cake is very moist and pale. It will dry completely on standing and the color will darken.) This cake is best when prepared several hours ahead or the day before serving.

Makes 1 cake

SWEET POTATO–APPLE CAKE

Here is a luscious way to use leftover sweet potatoes and applesauce—or maybe the best reason to make them in the first place. This cake keeps well, and when served with a scoop of vanilla ice cream, it's just wonderful.

3 tablespoons graham cracker crumbs
1½ cups unbleached white flour
1 cup whole wheat flour
2 teaspoons baking soda
1 teaspoon ground cinnamon
½ teaspoon ground cloves
¼ teaspoon ground cardamom
½ teaspoon salt
¾ cup vegetable oil
1¼ cups packed brown sugar
2 eggs, at room temperature
1¼ cups cooked, mashed, sweet potatoes
2 tablespoons lemon juice
1 cup unsweetened applesauce
1 cup raisins, soaked in rum (optional), drained

Grease a 10-inch microwavable tube pan or a 10- to 12-cup microwavable bundt pan. Sprinkle with graham crumbs, turning the pan to coat all the surfaces well and evenly.

In a medium bowl, sift together the flours, baking soda, cinnamon, cloves, cardamom, and salt. In a large bowl, beat the oil and sugar together until smooth. Beat in the eggs, one at a time, then beat in the sweet potatoes, lemon juice, and applesauce until thoroughly combined, scraping down the sides of the bowl once or twice. Gradually add the flour mixture to the egg mixture, stirring well. Fold in the raisins. Pour the batter into the prepared pan, smoothing with the back of a spoon.

Place the pan in the oven on an inverted microwavable cereal bowl or rack. Microwave on MEDIUM for 9 minutes, rotating once during cooking. Microwave on

HIGH for 4 to 8 minutes, or until a toothpick inserted in the center comes out clean. Rotate twice during cooking. Be careful not to overcook. Let the cake stand on a heat-resistant surface for 15 minutes, with a knife, loosen cake from side of pan. Place a serving plate over the pan and invert. Firmly tap the bottom of the pan, gently unmold, and let the cake cool. (Don't be concerned if the cake is very moist and pale. It will dry completely and the color will darken on standing.)

Makes 1 cake

COCOA BROWNIES

Brownies seem to be a special treat for just about everyone, so how could I not give a recipe for them? Using a round pan gives the best and most uniform results.

½ cup vegetable oil
½ cup Hershey's cocoa
1 cup sugar
2 eggs, at room temperature
1½ teaspoons vanilla extract
1 cup unbleached white flour
¼ teaspoon baking powder
¼ teaspoon salt (optional)
1 cup walnuts, coarsely chopped

Lightly grease a 9-inch round microwavable baking pan or glass pie plate.

In a medium microwavable bowl, combine the vegetable oil and cocoa; stir until smooth. Stir in the sugar. Add the eggs and vanilla; beat well. Stir in the flour, baking powder, salt, if desired, and nuts. Spread the batter in the prepared pan.

Microwave on MEDIUM for 7 minutes, rotating a quarter turn every 2 minutes. Microwave on HIGH for 1 to 3 minutes, or until the brownies begin to puff on

(continued)

(continued)

top. (Do not microwave until completely dry on top; a 1-inch wet spot should remain in the center.) Cover with aluminum foil. Let stand on a heat-resistant surface for 20 minutes. Remove the foil, place the pan on a rack and cool completely. Cut into wedges and serve.

Makes 8 to 10 servings

RHUBARB-PEAR CRISP

Rhubarb is wonderful on its own and combines beautifully with many other fruits. Firm Bosc pears, raisins, and rhubarb make a lovely trio for this homey dessert. Feel free to substitute granola for the crumb topping or to peel pears, if you prefer. But do use the food processor if you make the topping from scratch; it really improves the blend.

• •

1 cup rolled oats
½ cup whole wheat flour
⅓ cup packed brown sugar
1 teaspoon ground cinnamon
¼ teaspoon ground nutmeg
⅓ cup walnuts, coarsely chopped
6 tablespoons unsalted butter, chilled and cut into 6 pieces
1½ pounds rhubarb, trimmed and cut into 1-inch pieces (4 cups)
2 medium, firm, ripe Bosc pears, cored and cut into 1-inch pieces (2 cups)
⅓ cup raisins or currants
¼ cup pear nectar
2 teaspoons ground Minute tapioca (see Note)

• •

In the workbowl of a food processor, combine the oats, flour, sugar, cinnamon, and nutmeg. Process for 10 seconds until the ingredients are blended. Add the nuts and butter. Pulse several times until just combined and the mixture is crumbly. Set aside or cover and refrigerate until ready to use.

• •

•••

In a 2-quart microwavable baking dish, combine the rhubarb, pears, raisins, nectar, and tapioca. Sprinkle the topping over the fruits. Microwave, uncovered, on HIGH for 10 to 12 minutes, or until the fruit is tender and the topping is just bubbling. Let stand for 10 minutes. Serve warm or at room temperature.

Makes 6 to 8 servings

N O T E : Grinding tapioca in a blender or food processor will ensure that it dissolves completely in any method of cooking, microwave or conventional. Do a box at a time when you first buy it, then store in a cool dry place in an airtight container.

PEACH PANDOWDY

A version of this heirloom dessert that I enjoyed in a restaurant turned out to be perfect for adapting to the microwave. It is ideal for setting up before dinner and cooking in less time than it takes to clear the table. The piece of bread on the top acts as a "lid" and keeps the cream from melting into the dessert.

•••

½ cup peach nectar
3 tablespoons dark rum
2 tablespoons packed brown sugar, or to taste
2 teaspoons lemon juice
1 teaspoon finely chopped ginger
4 medium peaches, peeled and thinly sliced
8 slices Italian bread, ¼ inch thick, lightly buttered and toasted
Whipped cream, for garnish
Mint sprigs, for garnish

•••

In a medium bowl, combine the nectar, rum, sugar, lemon juice, and ginger; add the peaches and stir. Cover and let stand for 1 hour if time permits. Taste and adjust for sweetness, depending on the ripeness of the peaches.

(continued)

•••

(continued)

Place 1 slice of the toasted bread on the bottom of each of four 10-ounce soufflé dishes. Divide the peaches and liquid evenly among them. Place the soufflé dishes on a round microwave plate in a circle. Microwave on HIGH for 5 to 7 minutes, or until the peaches are tender and heated through.

Place the remaining bread on top of each dish. Top with freshly whipped cream and garnish with sprig of mint.

Makes 4 servings

PIE CRUSTS

There are lots of variations of pie crusts. Pressed pie crusts, using cookie crumbs, are about the simplest. Since they also have some color, your crust won't be pale, which is usual with microwave pie crusts. Here are the basic proportions for nine- and ten-inch pie crusts. Recipes may vary for thicker or richer crusts, but this will get you started. Chopped nuts can be substituted for up to half of the crumbs; decrease the shortening a bit in that case. Whirl your favorite cookie or cracker in a food processor or blender for a nice fine crumb.

4 tablespoons butter or margarine
2 to 3 tablespoons sugar or packed brown sugar (see Note)
1¼ cups finely crushed crumbs, from graham crackers, vanilla wafers, chocolate wafers, gingersnaps, or amaretti cookies
¼ teaspoon ground spices, such as nutmeg, cinnamon, etc. (optional)

Place the butter and sugar in a 9- or 10-inch microwavable pie plate. Microwave on HIGH for 1 minute, or until the butter is melted. Stir in the cookie crumbs and spices, if desired. Press the mixture firmly and evenly into the bottom and up the sides of the plate. Microwave on HIGH for 1½ to 2 minutes, or until the crust is set, rotating the plate once during cooking. Cool before filling.

Makes one 9-inch crust

CRANBERRY LINZER TART

The thick, rich cookie base of this tart will remind you of Linzer bars. Set this recipe up in a nine-inch square dish if you prefer, shielding the corners with aluminum foil for the initial baking. I try to keep cranberries in the freezer and surprise guests in the middle of summer. But whatever the season, this tart is always a pleasure. Serve it with a dollop of freshly whipped cream or vanilla ice cream when you're in the mood to splurge.

⅔ cup pecan pieces
⅔ cup whole wheat flour
⅔ cup unbleached white flour
1½ cups sugar, divided
½ cup (1 stick) unsalted butter
1 tablespoon grated orange peel, orange part only
1 tablespoon unsweetened cocoa powder
1 teaspoon ground cinnamon
¾ teaspoon ground cloves
1 12-ounce package fresh or frozen cranberries
¼ cup water
3 tablespoons orange juice
½ teaspoon almond extract
⅓ cup coarsely chopped pecans, toasted (page 24)

In a food processor, whirl the pecans until finely ground. Add the whole wheat and white flours, ½ cup of the sugar, the butter, orange peel, cocoa, cinnamon, and cloves.

(continued)

(continued)

Pulse the ingredients together until combined, stopping once or twice to scrape down the sides of the workbowl. Press the mixture firmly and evenly into the bottom and up the sides of a lightly greased 9-inch glass pie plate or cake dish. Microwave on HIGH for 5 minutes, rotating every 1 to 2 minutes. (Pat the crust down with the back of a spoon or rubber spatula if it puffs up.) Set the crust aside to cool.

In a deep 3-quart microwavable casserole, combine the cranberries, the remaining 1 cup of the sugar, water, orange juice, and almond extract. Microwave on HIGH for 12 to 16 minutes, or until the mixture has thickened considerably and is the consistency of jam, stirring occasionally. Let cool slightly. Spoon the cranberry mixture into the crust; sprinkle with the pecans. Cool on a rack until the filling sets. Refrigerate until ready to serve.

Makes 10 servings

SUMMER FRUIT TART

Recipes from the Good Housekeeping microwave kitchen have to be attractive since many of them are photographed. This tart, one of their creations, is as delicious as it is pretty. With berries and kiwi, there's no doubt that summer has arrived.

6 tablespoons butter or margarine
3 tablespoons packed dark brown sugar
1¼ cups vanilla-wafer crumbs (see Note)
½ cup sugar
2 tablespoons cornstarch
2 cups half-and-half
3 egg yolks
1½ teaspoons vanilla
8 medium strawberries, hulled and cut in half
1 kiwi, peeled and sliced
½ pint blueberries

Place the butter and sugar in a 9-inch microwavable pie plate. Microwave on HIGH for 1½ minutes or until the butter is melted. Stir in the vanilla wafer crumbs. Press the mixture firmly and evenly into the bottom and up the sides of the pie plate. Microwave on HIGH for 1 minute. Cool.

Meanwhile, in a 1-quart microwavable bowl, combine the sugar and cornstarch. Whisk in the half-and-half and the egg yolks. Microwave on HIGH for 5 to 6 minutes, or until thickened. Stir every 2 minutes. Add the vanilla; whisk until smooth. Pour into the crumb-lined pie plate. Gently press a sheet of plastic wrap directly onto the surface of the custard, to prevent a skin from forming. Refrigerate for 2 hours or until set. Remove the plastic wrap, arrange the fruits on the pie.

Makes 8 servings

N O T E : For 1¼ cups vanilla wafer crumbs, place 30 vanilla wafers in a food processor or blender and whirl until finely crushed.

PUMPKIN CHEESECAKE PIE

Joyce Kenneally, a friend who works at the Good Housekeeping Institute believes that cheesecake is one of the simplest desserts when made in the microwave. This version is especially festive a Thanksgiving or holiday meal.

4 tablespoons butter or margarine
1 cup gingersnap crumbs
½ cup pecans or walnuts, finely chopped
¾ cup plus 1 tablespoon packed brown sugar, divided
1 8-ounce package cream cheese
1 16-ounce can pumpkin
1 teaspoon vanilla
½ teaspoon ground cinnamon
1 envelope unflavored gelatin
½ cup milk
1 cup heavy cream

(continued)

(continued)

Place the butter in a 9-inch glass pie plate. Microwave on HIGH for 1 to 1½ minutes, or until melted. Stir in the gingersnap crumbs, pecans, and 1 tablespoon of the brown sugar. Press the mixture firmly and evenly into the bottom and up the sides of the pie plate. Microwave on HIGH for 1 minute, or until set, rotating once. Cool.

Meanwhile, place the unwrapped cream cheese in a large microwavable bowl. Microwave on MEDIUM-LOW for 1½ to 3 minutes, or until softened. Stir until smooth. Beat in the pumpkin, the remaining ¾ cup of brown sugar, vanilla, and cinnamon. In a 1-cup glass measure, sprinkle the gelatin over the milk; let stand for 1 minute and stir. Microwave on MEDIUM for 3 to 4½ minutes, or until the gelatin dissolves, stirring twice. Stir into the pumpkin mixture. Refrigerate for 30 to 45 minutes, until the mixture mounds when dropped from a spoon. Stir the mixture occasionally. Beat the heavy cream to soft peaks; fold into the pumpkin mixture. Spoon into the pie crust. Refrigerate for 3 hours, or until set, before serving.

Makes 8 to 10 servings

PUMPKIN-TOFU PIE

This cholesterol-free pie is also low in fat and gets some extra protein from tofu. Use whole eggs instead of just the whites if you prefer a richer dessert. Use any of the microwave Pie Crusts (pages 182–183). This dessert is a possible alternative to the Pumpkin Cheesecake Pie for the holidays.

4 tablespoons margarine
¾ cup gingersnap crumbs
¾ cup graham cracker crumbs
½ cup plus 2 tablespoons packed brown sugar, divided
2 10½-ounce packages soft tofu, drained
2 egg whites
1 tablespoon molasses (optional)
1½ cups canned pumpkin (not pumpkin pie mix)
2 tablespoons unbleached white flour

2 teaspoons ground cinnamon
½ teaspoon ground allspice
½ teaspoon ground nutmeg
½ teaspoon ground ginger
1 teaspoon vanilla

Place the margarine in a 9-inch glass pie plate. Microwave on HIGH for 1 to 1½ minutes, or until melted. Stir in the crumbs and 2 tablespoons of the brown sugar. Press the mixture firmly and evenly into the bottom and up the sides of the pie plate. Microwave on HIGH for 1 minute, or until set, rotating once. Cool.

Meanwhile, in a food processor, blend the remaining ½ cup of brown sugar, the tofu, egg whites, molasses, if desired, pumpkin, flour, cinnamon, allspice, nutmeg, ginger, and vanilla together until thoroughly combined, stopping to scrape down the sides of the workbowl once or twice. Pour the filling into a 2-quart glass measure or bowl. Microwave on HIGH for 2 to 4 minutes, or until heated through, stirring once during cooking. Pour into the baked pie shell. Microwave on MEDIUM for 10 to 12 minutes, or until almost set (and the center jiggles slightly), rotating twice during cooking. Let stand for 30 minutes.

Chill for at least 3 hours and serve.

Makes 8 servings

LOMBARDY CUSTARD

A recipe from food historian Lorna J. Sass, this spicy fruited custard was served at King Richard II's feast given with the Duke of Lancaster on September 23, 1387. The sweetness of the dried fruits is contrasted in an unusual and pleasant way with fresh parsley. Transferring a frozen pie shell into a glass pie plate is a quick way to pull this together.

1 uncooked pie shell (9 inches)
3 eggs, lightly beaten
1 cup heavy cream
2 tablespoons packed brown sugar
1 teaspoon ground cinnamon
¾ teaspoon dried orange peel
Pinch salt
Pinch mace
10 dried prunes, pitted and cut into small pieces
10 dried dates, pitted and cut into small pieces
10 dried figs, cut into small pieces
3 tablespoons finely minced parsley
2 tablespoons unsalted butter, cut into small pieces

Prick the pie shell with a fork on the bottom and sides at ½-inch intervals. Microwave on HIGH for 4 to 7 minutes, or until the crust appears dry and opaque (remember it will not brown in the microwave). Rotate a half turn every 2 minutes. Set aside and let cool.

In a 2-cup glass measure, combine the eggs, cream, sugar, cinnamon, orange peel, salt, and mace with a wire whisk until well blended. Microwave on HIGH for 2 minutes, stirring after 1 minute.

Line the pie crust with the dried fruits; distribute the parsley and butter evenly over the fruits. Pour the egg mixture over the fruits. Microwave on MEDIUM for 12 to 14 minutes, or until the filling is just set and the center jiggles slightly. Rotate every 3 minutes while cooking. Let stand on heat-resistant surface for 20 minutes.

Makes 8 servings

MOLASSES CORN PUDDING

This dessert may remind you of Indian pudding, a traditional New England dessert. Use a good unsulphured molasses for full flavor, or honey for a milder taste. A true Indian pudding should stand for about half an hour to set slightly, but this version is so fragrant and tempting that you may not be able to wait that long.

3 cups milk
⅓ cup unsulphured molasses
⅓ cup yellow cornmeal
3 tablespoons unsalted butter
¾ teaspoon ground ginger
½ teaspoon ground cinnamon
¼ teaspoon ground nutmeg
¼ teaspoon salt
3 eggs, well beaten

In an oval 2-quart microwavable casserole, stir together the milk and molasses. (The molasses need not dissolve completely.) Microwave, uncovered, on HIGH for 4 to 6 minutes, or until very hot and almost boiling. Slowly stir in the cornmeal, then stir in the butter, ginger, cinnamon, nutmeg, and salt. Microwave on HIGH for 3 to 5 minutes, or until slightly thickened, stirring once. Slowly whisk the eggs into the cornmeal mixture. Microwave on MEDIUM for 15 to 18 minutes, or until the center is almost set, and a knife inserted 1 inch from the center comes out clean. Let stand for 10 minutes. Serve warm.

Makes 4 servings

STEAMED DATE PUDDING

Pears, dates, and currants make for a delectable dessert here. No water bath is needed for microwave steamed puddings and they cook in a fraction of the conventional cooking time. This dessert is more than delicious—it's high in fiber, B vitamins, and iron.

3 medium Bosc pears, peeled, cored, and diced (about 1½ pounds)
2 teaspoons lemon juice
1 cup coarsely chopped dates
½ cup currants
¾ cup coarsely chopped walnuts
1½ cups whole wheat pastry flour
1 cup sugar
1 teaspoon baking powder
1½ teaspoons ground cinnamon
1 teaspoon ground allspice
3 eggs
½ cup vegetable oil
1 teaspoon vanilla
Vanilla Sauce, (pages 211–212) (optional)

Grease a 10- to 12-cup microwavable bundt pan; set aside.

In a medium mixing bowl, combine the pears and lemon juice; set aside. In a large bowl, combine the dates, currants, and walnuts. Combine the flour, sugar, baking powder, cinnamon, and allspice and sift over the dried fruits and nuts and toss until well combined.

In a small bowl, beat the eggs, oil, and vanilla; add to the pears and stir to combine. Pour over the flour mixture and stir thoroughly, then pour into the prepared pan. Cover tightly with vented plastic wrap. Microwave on MEDIUM-HIGH for 14 to 17 minutes, or until a tester inserted in the middle comes out clean and the pudding slightly pulls away from the sides of the pan, rotating the pan once after 5 minutes.

Let stand, covered, on a heat-resistant surface for 15 minutes. Gently loosen the sides of the pudding and invert onto a serving plate.

Serve warm with vanilla sauce, if desired.

Makes 8 to 10 servings

N O T E : You can also prepare this in a 6-cup ring mold. Add 5 to 7 minutes to the cooking time, testing for doneness as indicated.

AMASAKE PUDDING

Amasake is a fermented rice product that releases the sweetness of brown rice into a liquid. This rich nectar, found in the refrigerator at most health-food stores, is sold plain and flavored. Brands vary in thickness and in taste; try a few to find your favorite. I like to use almond amasake with Cream of Wheat for a toothsome dessert.

2 cups water
1½ cups almond amasake
⅔ cup Cream of Wheat
½ cup raisins
2 tablespoons packed brown sugar
1 teaspoon ground cinnamon
¼ cup sliced almonds, toasted (page 24)

In a 3-quart microwavable casserole, combine the water, amasake, cereal, raisins, sugar, and cinnamon. Microwave on HIGH for 6 to 8 minutes, or until thickened, stirring every 2 minutes. Let stand for 1 minute. Spoon into small dessert dishes; sprinkle with toasted almonds and serve.

Makes 4 to 6 servings

N O T E : Amasake is dairy-free. Use Cream of Rice for a dessert that is wheat-free as well.

RICH RICE PUDDING

This is the classic rice pudding to make, with total abandon, when you long for a creamy, dreamy comfort food. Though I prefer it warm, there are lots of folks, like my neighbor Barbara, who say that chilled is the only way to go.

1 cup heavy cream
1 cup milk
2 egg yolks, at room temperature
3 tablespoons sugar
1¼ teaspoons vanilla
½ teaspoon almond extract
¼ teaspoon freshly grated nutmeg
2 cups cooked rice (page 260)
¼ cup sliced almonds, toasted (page 24) for garnish (optional)

In a 3-quart microwavable casserole, whisk together the cream, milk, egg yolks, sugar, vanilla, almond extract, and nutmeg until thoroughly combined and no streaks of egg yolk remain.

Stir in the cooked rice. Cover tightly with lid or vented plastic wrap. Microwave on MEDIUM for 5 to 9 minutes, or until very hot and just boiling; stir.

Re-cover and microwave on MEDIUM-LOW for 15 to 20 minutes, or until thick and creamy, stirring every 4 minutes. Let stand, covered, for 10 minutes. (The pudding will thicken a bit more on standing.)

Spoon the pudding into small dessert dishes. Sprinkle with toasted almonds, if desired.

Makes 4 to 6 servings

NOTE: Eggs are easier to separate when they are still cold, but they blend better when they are at room temperature. Store unused egg whites in the freezer for future use.

RICE PUDDING

Using short-grain rice for this pudding will give you a creamy consistency without the egg yolks or heavy cream found in the more classic version. To reheat, add a bit of milk to restore the creamy texture.

2 cups water
1 cup short-grain or Arborio rice
2 cups half-and-half or milk
½ cup sugar
1 teaspoon vanilla
¼ cup raisins
2 tablespoons dark rum

In an oval 3-quart microwavable casserole, combine the water and rice. Cover with a lid or vented plastic wrap. Microwave on HIGH for 3 to 5 minutes, or until just boiling. Reduce the setting to MEDIUM and cook for 7 to 9 minutes, or until most of the liquid is absorbed.

Stir in the half-and-half, sugar, and vanilla. Re-cover and microwave on HIGH for 2 minutes. Reduce setting to MEDIUM-LOW and cook for 10 minutes. Stir, re-cover and microwave on MEDIUM-LOW for 15 to 18 minutes, or until thickened, stirring every 4 minutes. Add the raisins and rum. (The mixture will still be soupy, but it will thicken on standing.) Re-cover and let stand for 10 minutes before serving.

Makes 6 servings

GOLDEN APPLE BREAD PUDDING

Using a whole grain or wheat bread gives this pudding a nutty taste and firmer texture than usual. Golden Delicious apples are especially nice here, but feel free to use your favorite variety.

3 cups milk
3 eggs, at room temperature
¾ cup packed brown sugar
1½ teaspoons vanilla
½ teaspoon ground cinnamon
¼ teaspoon ground nutmeg
8 slices whole wheat bread, slightly stale
2 medium Golden Delicious apples, peeled, cored, and thinly sliced (about 1 pound)
½ cup golden raisins
2 tablespoons butter, cut into small pieces

In a 1-quart glass measure, heat the milk on HIGH for 2 minutes. In a large bowl, beat the eggs; whisk in the sugar, vanilla, cinnamon, and nutmeg. Gradually whisk in the warm milk. Microwave on MEDIUM for 2 minutes, or until heated through. Stir, making sure that the sugar has completely dissolved.

Meanwhile, cut the bread into halves or quarters. Arrange 1 layer of bread in a lightly buttered 2-quart oval casserole. Arrange a layer of apples on top and sprinkle with a few raisins. Pour about half of the egg mixture on top. Continue with the remaining bread, finishing with an apple layer and some of the custard poured over the top. Cover loosely with plastic wrap. Let stand for 20 minutes so the bread can absorb some of the custard.

Microwave on HIGH for 3 minutes. Reduce setting to MEDIUM-HIGH and microwave for 15 minutes. Rotate once during cooking. Uncover, place butter over the top, and microwave on MEDIUM-HIGH, uncovered, for 6 to 9 minutes, or until a knife inserted 1 inch from the center comes out clean.

Makes 6 servings

STEPHEN'S BREAD PUDDING

Master Recipes is an impressive volume that makes the art of cooking simple. Author Stephen Schmidt was gracious enough to share this recipe along with a tip on nutmeg that follows. Stephen suggests serving this with warm or chilled heavy cream; I like some warm maple syrup poured over the top.

⅔ cup raisins
⅓ cup dark rum or brandy
2 cups milk
1 cup light cream
4 to 5 cups crustless bread crumbs (about 12 ounces)
2 eggs
¾ cup sugar
1½ teaspoons freshly grated nutmeg or ¾ teaspoon ground nutmeg
¼ teaspoon salt
2 tablespoons butter, cut into small pieces
Heavy cream or maple syrup (optional)

In a small bowl, combine the raisins and rum; set aside. Pour the milk and cream into a 4-cup glass measure. Microwave on HIGH for 3 to 4 minutes, or until heated through (do not allow to boil). In a large bowl, combine the heated milk and bread crumbs. Let stand for 30 minutes.

In a medium bowl, whisk together the eggs, sugar, nutmeg, and salt until light. Fold the egg mixture and raisins and liquor into the bread.

Pour the pudding into a lightly buttered 2-quart oval casserole. Scatter the butter pieces over the top. Microwave on HIGH for 3 minutes. Reduce the setting to MEDIUM and microwave for 15 to 18 minutes, or until the pudding has puffed and a knife inserted 1 inch from the center comes out clean. Rotate once during cooking. Let stand for 5 minutes.

Serve with heavy cream or maple syrup, if desired.

Makes 4 to 6 servings

STOCKS AND SAUCES

Basic Vegetable Stock
Tomato Vegetable Stock
Mushroom Stock
Tomato Sauce with Fennel and Mint
Chunky Tomato Sauce
Shocking Pink Pasta Sauce
Fresh Mushroom Sauce
Red Pepper Sauce
Spicy Peanut Sauce
Sharon's White Sauce
Clarified Butter
Tahini Sauce
Mustard Sauce
Horseradish-Yogurt Sauce
Yogurt-Cucumber Dressing
Vanilla Sauce
Lemon Sauce
Hattie's Cranberry Sauce

Sauces are incredibly easy to prepare in the microwave oven. You will become spoiled when you discover how fast and simple they can be. Even sauces that usually need to be stirred and watched on top of the stove are prepared with a minimum of fuss in the microwave.

Sauces can greatly enhance the flavor and the presentation of many foods. Vegetable sauces, especially, lend contrast and color without contributing extra fat calories. Whether the sauce is a topping for pasta or a dipping sauce for vegetables, I'm sure you'll be delighted when you discover how convenient it is to make.

Not all of the recipes are for cooked sauces. The uncooked ones are nice to put together at the last minute or when you have some chilled leftover vegetables on hand. The Horseradish-Yogurt Sauce is perfect at such times and the Mustard Sauce is as good on eggs as it is on vegetables. When you keep the mix for Sharon's White Sauce in your pantry, a low-cal, no-fat sauce is ready in just about one minute flat.

BASIC VEGETABLE STOCK

Vary this basic recipe with whatever you have on hand or whatever vegetables are in season. Feel free to eliminate the oil in the initial stage if you like. Instead, add a few tablespoons of water to the casserole with the onions, cover tightly, and "sweat" them for full flavor. Increase the cooking time to an hour or more for a richer stock.

2 tablespoons olive oil (optional)
1 large onion, coarsely chopped
2 medium carrots with greens, scrubbed and sliced
2 medium parsnips, scrubbed and sliced
2 celery ribs, with leaves, sliced
1 medium turnip, peeled (about 6 ounces)
1 medium zucchini, sliced (about 8 ounces)
6 sprigs parsley
1 teaspoon chopped thyme or ½ teaspoon dried thyme
6 black peppercorns
1 bay leaf
Pinch ground nutmeg
6 cups water
Salt to taste

In a 5-quart microwavable casserole, combine the oil and onions (or sprinkle the onion with 3 tablespoons of water if a fat-free stock is preferred). Microwave on HIGH for 3 minutes. Add the remaining ingredients, except the salt, and stir. Cover tightly with a lid or vented plastic wrap. Microwave on HIGH for 10 to 12 minutes, or until boiling. Stir and partially re-cover. Microwave on MEDIUM for 30 to 40 minutes to develop flavor. Rotate the casserole once during cooking. Let stand, covered, for 10 minutes. Cool slightly.

Strain the stock into a bowl, gently pressing the liquid out of the vegetables with the back of a spoon. Let cool, add salt to taste, and store in a covered container in the refrigerator or freezer (will keep up to six months).

Makes about 5 cups

TOMATO VEGETABLE STOCK

Tomatoes lend vegetable stock their own special flavor, which is better in certain dishes. Mike Center developed this one to go with his corn chowder (page 55).

2 tablespoons butter or oil
5 garlic cloves, peeled and crushed
1 medium onion, coarsely chopped
6 cups water
4 plum tomatoes, coarsely chopped
4 carrots, scrubbed and coarsely chopped
4 celery ribs, with leaves, coarsely chopped
8 springs parsley, coarsely chopped
½ teaspoon salt
½ teaspoon freshly ground black pepper

In a 3-quart microwavable casserole, combine the butter or oil, garlic, and onion. Cover tightly with a lid or vented plastic wrap. Microwave on HIGH for 3 minutes, stirring once. Stir in water, tomatoes, carrots, celery, parsley, salt, and pepper. Cover loosely and microwave on HIGH for 40 minutes, rotating once. Cool slightly.

Strain the stock into a bowl, gently pressing the liquid out of the vegetables with the back of a spoon.

Transfer the vegetables to a food processor or blender. Add 1 cup of the stock and puree. Strain the liquid back into the stock; discard the remaining vegetables. Store in a covered container in the refrigerator or freezer.

Makes about 6 cups

MUSHROOM STOCK

A good mushroom stock is a pleasant change from vegetable broths. It's a nice addition to pilafs, casseroles, and soups. The oil can be eliminated by adding one half cup of the water with the leeks and garlic and proceeding. This stock is so good you may want to serve it as a zesty mushroom soup with some tofu chunks added for protein. Be warned, however: My sister comments that as a soup, "It's begging for croutons and melted cheese."

2 tablespoons vegetable oil
2 medium leeks, white parts only, thinly sliced
2 garlic cloves, chopped
10 sliced fresh mushrooms (about 8 ounces)
2 dried mushrooms, broken into pieces (about 1 ounce)
4 sprigs parsley
1 sage leaf or ¼ teaspoon dried sage leaves
5 black peppercorns
5 allspice berries
6 cups water
Salt to taste

In a 3-quart microwavable casserole, combine the oil, leeks, and garlic (or combine the leeks and garlic with ½ cup of the water). Microwave on HIGH for 3 minutes. Add the remaining ingredients, except the salt, and stir. Cover tightly with a lid or vented plastic wrap. Microwave on HIGH for 10 to 12 minutes, or until boiling. Stir and partially re-cover. Microwave on MEDIUM for 25 minutes to develop flavor. Rotate the casserole once during cooking. Let stand, covered, for 10 minutes.

Strain the stock into a bowl, gently pressing the liquid out of the vegetables with the back of a spoon. Let cool, add salt to taste, and store in a covered container in the refrigerator or freezer.

Makes 6 cups

TOMATO SAUCE WITH FENNEL AND MINT

This sauce is especially nice in summer when all of the ingredients are fresh. If the tomatoes are too acidic, a little sugar will round out the flavors; Toss the sauce with fresh pasta, serve it with the Lasagne Florentine Rolls (pages 96–97), or even use it as the steaming liquid for fresh vegetables. By all means double the recipe; it freezes beautifully.

2 tablespoons olive oil
2 garlic cloves, minced
2 pounds ripe tomatoes, coarsely chopped, or 2 cups canned Italian plum tomatoes, with juices
2 tablespoons chopped parsley
2 tablespoons chopped basil or 1 tablespoon dried basil
2 tablespoons chopped mint or 2 teaspoons dried mint
¼ teaspoon fennel seeds, crushed
Sugar (optional)
Salt and freshly ground black pepper to taste

In a 3-quart microwavable casserole, combine the oil and garlic. Microwave on HIGH for 1 minute. Stir in the tomatoes. Microwave on HIGH, uncovered, for 9 minutes; stir and rotate once during cooking. (Break up the tomatoes with the back of a spoon if using canned.) Stir in the parsley, basil, mint, fennel, and a bit of sugar, if desired. Microwave on MEDIUM, uncovered, for 8 to 10 minutes, or until the tomatoes are soft to chunky in consistency. Stir and rotate once during cooking. (Don't worry if the sauce is too thin, it will thicken on standing.) Let stand for 5 minutes before serving. Add additional sugar, if needed, and salt and pepper to taste.

Makes 3 cups

NOTE: I rarely peel tomatoes for sauce. If you prefer a smoother consistency, peel the tomatoes and reduce the cooking time slightly. (To peel tomatoes, drop them in boiling water for 1 minute; remove with a slotted spoon and transfer to a bowl of cold water. This helps the skins to slip off easily.) You can also cool the sauce and put it through a food mill or pulse it several times in a food processor.

CHUNKY TOMATO SAUCE

A freshly cooked sauce can make the simplest dish a really special one. As long as there are ripe tomatoes to be found, make your sauce from scratch. This version is the one used for the lasagne recipes in this book, but you'll find that it goes well with many other pasta, grain, and bean dishes as well.

3 tablespoons olive oil
1 medium onion, coarsely chopped
3 garlic cloves, minced
3 pounds ripe tomatoes, chopped, or 4 cups canned whole tomatoes, with juices
3 tablespoons chopped parsley
1½ teaspoons sugar, or to taste
2 tablespoons chopped oregano, or 2 teaspoons dried oregano, crumbled
2 tablespoons chopped basil, or 1 tablespoon dried basil, crumbled
½ teaspoon dried thyme, crumbled
¼ teaspoon freshly ground black pepper
Salt to taste

In a 3-quart microwavable casserole, combine the oil, onion, and garlic. Microwave on HIGH for 3 to 4 minutes, or until the onion is tender. Stir in the tomatoes. (Break up the tomatoes with the back of a spoon, if using canned.) Microwave on HIGH for 6 minutes, or until the sauce is just boiling. Add parsley, sugar, oregano, basil, thyme, and pepper, stirring well to combine. Microwave on HIGH for 8 minutes, or until the sauce is thickened slightly. Rotate and stir once during cooking. Let stand for 5 minutes before serving. Adjust seasonings, adding salt to taste.

Makes about 6 cups

N O T E : If a smoother sauce is desired, cool slightly and put through a food mill or pulse several times in a food processor.

SHOCKING PINK PASTA SAUCE

Start your guests with appetizer portions of pasta with this sauce. Its pink hue is most unusual, quite a difference from the red sauces to which they are accustomed. A cooked red beet gives a vibrant color to this sauce, and red wine lends a hearty flavor. One taste and folks plead for more. Don't just use it for pasta, though; it's wonderful on vegetables and can be served hot or cold.

1 small onion, thinly sliced
2 tablespoons butter
2 tablespoons olive oil
½ cup dry red wine
1 medium red beet, cooked, peeled, and diced
½ cup half-and-half
1 tablespoon lemon juice
¼ cup grated Parmesan cheese
Salt and freshly ground black pepper to taste
12 basil leaves, shredded, for garnish

In a 1-quart microwavable casserole, combine the onion, butter, and oil. Microwave on HIGH for 2 minutes, or until the onion is tender. Add the wine and beet. Microwave on HIGH for 2 to 3 minutes, or until just boiling. Cool slightly.

Puree the beet mixture in a food processor or blender until smooth. Add the half-and-half, lemon juice, and cheese; blend until combined. Add salt and pepper to taste.

Return sauce to the casserole if serving hot. Re-cover and microwave on HIGH for 2 to 3 minutes, or until the sauce is heated through.

Pour over pasta or vegetables and garnish with shredded basil leaves.

Makes 1⅔ cups

FRESH MUSHROOM SAUCE

Whole grains enter a new dimension when this sauce is spooned on top. It's also nice over broccoli or for times when you're combining leftovers to make a quick main dish.

3 tablespoons olive oil
2 tablespoons unbleached white flour
1½ cups Basic Vegetable Stock (page 199) or Mushroom Stock (page 201)
1 tablespoon lemon juice
1 tablespoon dry vermouth
1½ cups sliced mushrooms (about 4 ounces)
2 tablespoons chopped parsley
⅛ teaspoon freshly ground black pepper
Salt to taste

Pour the oil into a 4-cup glass measure or 1-quart microwavable bowl. Microwave on HIGH for 1 to 2 minutes, or until very hot. Whisk in flour until smooth. Microwave on HIGH for 1 to 2 minutes, or until bubbly. Slowly whisk in the stock, lemon juice, and vermouth. Microwave on HIGH for 5 minutes, or until boiling, stirring once during cooking. Stir in mushrooms, parsley, and pepper. Microwave on HIGH for 6 minutes or until the sauce thickens, stirring every 2 minutes. Add salt to taste.

Makes 2½ cups

RED PEPPER SAUCE

You can steam the peppers separately in a plastic cooking bag, but I think that heating the ingredients together gives the sauce a richer flavor. Add a chopped serrano or jalapeño pepper if you like a spicy sauce. Serve it on green and white pasta for a vivid presentation.

4 medium red bell peppers, seeded and diced
½ cup chopped onion
2 shallots, minced
1 clove garlic, minced
3 tablespoons olive oil
½ cup Basic Vegetable Stock, (page 199) (optional)
½ teaspoon salt
¼ teaspoon freshly ground black pepper

In a 3-quart microwavable casserole, combine the peppers, onion, shallots, garlic, and oil. Toss well to coat with oil. Cover tightly with a lid or vented plastic wrap. Microwave on HIGH for 10 to 12 minutes, or until the peppers and onion are soft. Stir and rotate once during cooking. Let stand, covered, for 5 minutes. Cool slightly.

Puree the pepper mixture in a food processor or blender until smooth. Slowly pour in stock to thin the sauce, if desired. Add salt and pepper. Serve at room temperature.

Makes 2 cups

NOTE: The sauce also can be served hot. Return the sauce to the casserole, re-cover, and microwave on HIGH for 2 to 3 minutes, or until the sauce is heated through.

SPICY PEANUT SAUCE

I'm not sure there's anything I don't like with this sauce. Most times my guests have enjoyed it with vegetable platters, though it's a winner on pasta and with grains. Use it for the Asian Noodle Salad (pages 120–121).

¼ cup Basic Vegetable Stock (page 199) or Mushroom Stock (page 201)
2 garlic cloves, minced
2 teaspoons fresh ginger, finely chopped
2 teaspoons molasses
½ cup smooth peanut butter
2 tablespoons lime juice
¼ teaspoon ground red pepper

In a 4-cup glass measure, combine the stock, garlic, ginger, and molasses. Cover with vented plastic wrap. Microwave on HIGH for 3 minutes, or until boiling. Let stand for 2 minutes. Whisk in the peanut butter, lime juice, and red pepper.

Makes about 1 cup

SHARON'S WHITE SAUCE

When I was writing this book, my younger sister Sharon, a computer whiz, left this goodie on my disk. It is a rich-tasting nonfat white sauce. You'll never be without a sauce again when you keep the dry mix on your shelf. I add curry powder, tarragon, and dry mustard to taste for a whole repertoire of variations.

2 cups nonfat dry milk
1 cup unbleached white flour
Water
Salt to taste

(continued)

(continued)

In a small bowl, stir the dry milk and flour together until thoroughly combined. Store in an airtight container in a cool, dry place.

In a 2-cup measure, whisk 1 cup water and ⅓ cup of the sauce mix together until smooth. Microwave on HIGH for 1 minute, or until the sauce is thickened, stirring every 20 seconds. Add salt to taste.

Makes 3 cups of mix, 1 cup of sauce

CLARIFIED BUTTER

If you're a fan of Indian cooking, you're familiar with ghee, which is used in dals and other dishes. It is the clear, oily liquid that remains when butter is melted and the solids are skimmed off the top. It is a snap to make in the microwave.

½ pound (2 sticks) unsalted butter, each stick cut into quarters

Put the butter chunks into a 4-cup glass measure; cover loosely with a paper towel or wax paper. Microwave on HIGH for 2 to 3 minutes, or until melted. Let stand for about 3 minutes to let the milk solids settle. Skim any remaining solids off the top. Carefully pour off the clear liquid into a container; discard the remaining white solids. Store, tightly covered, in the refrigerator.

Makes about ¾ cup

N O T E : You can also line a sieve with cheesecloth and pour the butter through into a container. Repeat if some residue remains.

TAHINI SAUCE

There's no cooking at all for this simple sauce, which whirls up in a blender. Tahini, or ground sesame seeds, is available in health-food stores. The sauce might get pasty if held in the refrigerator, but let it come to room temperature add a bit of water and stir, and it will be just fine. Pour it over green beans or cold vegetables for a great salad.

1 garlic clove, peeled
2 tablespoons tahini
2 tablespoons lemon juice
1 tablespoon balsamic vinegar
2 tablespoons sesame oil
⅓ cup vegetable oil
Salt and freshly ground black pepper to taste

Place the garlic, tahini, lemon juice, and vinegar in a blender. Blend until the garlic is pureed. With the motor running, slowly pour in the sesame and vegetable oils until just blended. Add salt and pepper to taste.

Makes about 1 cup

MUSTARD SAUCE

This no-cook mustard sauce is always ready to serve. Use it over omelets, vegetables, or serve as a dip, as well as with scallion bows (page 44). Add some thyme or tarragon for a subtle herb flavor.

½ cup plain yogurt
½ cup mayonnaise
¼ cup Dijon mustard
¼ teaspoon freshly ground white pepper, or to taste
Juice of 1 lime

In a small mixing bowl, whisk together the yogurt, mayonnaise, mustard, pepper, and lime. Cover and refrigerate until ready to serve.

Makes 1¼ cups

HORSERADISH-YOGURT SAUCE

A cool yet spicy sauce, this goes well with steamed vegetables or as a sandwich enhancer. Add some chopped herbs or a dash of Tabasco for variety.

1 cup plain yogurt
½ cup mayonnaise
2 tablespoons horseradish, or to taste
2 teaspoons lemon juice

In a small bowl, whisk together yogurt, mayonnaise, horseradish, and lemon juice. Cover and store in the refrigerator.

Makes about 1½ cups

YOGURT-CUCUMBER DRESSING

This chunky dressing is a refreshing topping for salads or chilled vegetables. Use it over fresh green beans and garnish with chopped red radishes for a really pretty presentation.

1⅓ cups plain yogurt
¼ cup mayonnaise
2 tablespoons lime juice
2 tablespoons chopped mint
1 tablespoon chopped parsley
⅛ teaspoon ground red pepper, or to taste
½ cup chopped cucumber

In a small bowl, whisk together the yogurt, mayonnaise, lime juice, mint, parsley, and red pepper; fold in cucumber until all the ingredients are well blended.

For a smoother sauce, place all ingredients in a food processor or blender; mix until just combined.

Makes about 2 cups

VANILLA SAUCE

Serve this dessert sauce over fresh fruits or Steamed Date Pudding (page 190).

1 cup half-and-half or milk
3 egg yolks
¼ cup sugar
1 teaspoon vanilla
1 teaspoon raspberry liqueur (optional)

(continued)

(continued)

Pour the to milk into a 4-cup glass measure. Microwave on HIGH for 1½ to 2 minutes, or until heated through.

In a small bowl, whisk the egg yolks and sugar until blended. Gradually whisk in about ¼ cup of the heated half-and-half to the egg yolk mixture, then return the egg yolk mixture to the remaining heated milk. Microwave on MEDIUM for 4 to 5 minutes, or until the mixture coats the back of a spoon, stirring 2 or 3 times. Stir in the vanilla and liqueur, if desired.

Cool slightly. Serve warm or cover and refrigerate for several hours or overnight.

Makes 1 cup

LEMON SAUCE

Here's the perfect sauce to spoon over fresh berries and angel food or pound cake.

⅓ cup sugar
1 tablespoon cornstarch
⅔ cup half-and-half or milk
1 egg yolk
2 tablespoons lemon juice
1 teaspoon grated lemon peel, yellow part only

In a 4-cup glass measure, combine the sugar and cornstarch. Whisk in the half-and-half, egg yolk, lemon juice, and lemon peel. Microwave on HIGH for 2 to 3 minutes, or until thickened, stirring twice.

Makes 1 cup

HATTIE'S CRANBERRY SAUCE

Hattie Harris is not only my sister Rita's partner and a fine lawyer, she's a great cook. She likes to serve her cranberry sauce as a relish with the main part of a meal, but I think it's sensational over vanilla ice cream. Truthfully, more often than not, I simply eat it out of the jar.

1 12-ounce bag fresh or frozen cranberries
1 cup plus 2 tablespoons granulated sugar or turbinado (see Note)
¾ cup water
¼ teaspoon vanilla
½ cup cognac

In a 3-quart microwavable casserole, combine the cranberries, 1 cup of the sugar, water, and half of the cognac. Cover with a lid or vented plastic wrap. Microwave on HIGH for 6 to 8 minutes (10 to 12 minutes if the cranberries are frozen), or until the sugar dissolves and the cranberries start to pop. Stir once during cooking.

Uncover, stir in vanilla and the remaining sugar and cognac. Let stand to cool. Store in a tightly covered container in the refrigerator.

Makes 4 cups

N O T E : Turbinado, a less refined sugar, is available in health-food stores.

EASY ENHANCEMENTS

Zucchini-Apple Butter
Dried Fruit Chutney
Santa Rosa Plum Preserves
Peach-Raspberry Jam
Autumn Harvest Fruit Spread
Yogurt
Savory Oat Bran Topping
Italian Rice Bran Topping
Spicy Sesame Seed Topper
Cocoa-Nut Topping
Coco Crunch Topping
Green Curry Paste
Hi-Fi Crunch
Garam Masala
Multigrain Mix

Easy enhancements are a new dimension for microwave users. These are recipes for foods that most people don't make from scratch in conventional cooking and probably would never consider doing so in the microwave. Now you can make homemade preserves and chutnies faster and easier than you've ever dreamed. Though the yogurt recipe takes some time, it is far creamier than any you have ever bought in a store, and it is virtually fat free!

In this chapter I have provided a selection of recipes for toppings. These are meant to give extra pizazz to foods, whether fresh or cooked. For instance, the Hi-Fi Crunch, made with rolled oats, rice bran, and sunflower seeds, is great stirred into yogurt for a light lunch or snack or sprinkled on top of hot breakfast cereal. Savory toppings go well with casseroles, pasta, and vegetables. They are especially good to use with biscuits and quick breads, which don't brown when made in the microwave. You can also use toasted nuts and seeds, such as almonds, walnuts, pecans, pine nuts, and sesame seeds, as toppings.

The Green Curry Paste and Garam Masala are especially popular with those who enjoy the flavors of Asian and Indian foods. These condiments can be tricky to find if a specialty store is not close by. Now you'll have a safe supply ready at a moment's notice. Take special note of the Multigrain Mix. This simple trick of combining a variety of grains has gotten more rave reviews than I can tell you. It's a way to give your grains a new personality.

Note that the fruit butter, preserves, and chutney recipes are not meant to be true canning or preserving recipes. They are a quick way to have unusual and freshly prepared foods that used to take hours to make. Here are a few pointers to get you started:

1. The United States Department of Agriculture (USDA) and the Ball Corporation are no longer recommending the use of paraffin for sealing jelly. You may see some microwave recipes that instruct you to use paraffin; no more.

2. Avoid old-fashioned closures. Use two-piece vacuum lids for best results.

3. Wash jars and lids in hot soapy water and rinse well. They can also be put through the dishwasher cycle and filled while still hot.

4. These recipes can be stored safely in the refrigerator for several weeks or in the freezer for several months. For longer storage and actual preserving, the USDA recommends that filled jars be placed on a rack in a boiling-water bath and boiled for 5 minutes. This process can not be done in the microwave.

5. Because of the high sugar content, boil-ups can occur. Use deep, generously sized casseroles to avoid this. The microwave oven eliminates the need for constant stirring and the risk of scorching and it's perfect for small batches. Large quantities are best done in a large kettle on top of the stove.

ZUCCHINI-APPLE BUTTER

Try this vegetable and fruit topping instead of butter for muffins, rolls, and toast. It has a nice spicy flavor that I find is great on whole wheat pancakes too.

3 medium zucchini, peeled and coarsely chopped (about 1¼ pounds)
1 large Granny Smith apple, peeled, cored, and coarsely chopped (about 8 ounces)
2 tablespoons lemon juice
2 tablespoons maple syrup
¼ cup packed brown sugar
1½ teaspoons ground cinnamon
½ teaspoon ground nutmeg
¼ teaspoon ground cloves

In a 3-quart microwavable casserole, combine the zucchini, apple, and lemon juice. Cover tightly with a lid or vented plastic wrap. Microwave on HIGH for 8 to 10 minutes, or until soft. Let stand, covered, for 3 minutes. Cool slightly.

Puree the zucchini mixture in a food processor or blender until smooth; return to the casserole. Add the maple syrup, brown sugar, cinnamon, nutmeg, and cloves; stir thoroughly to combine. Microwave on HIGH for 3 to 5 minutes, or until boiling; stir. Microwave on MEDIUM for 8 to 10 minutes, or until the mixture has thickened, stirring once during cooking.

Spoon into hot clean jars and cover tightly. Store in the refrigerator for about 1 month.

Makes 2 cups

DRIED FRUIT CHUTNEY

I started making this chutney routinely after a friend gave it to me for Christmas. Since it uses dried fruits, this juicy condiment can be made at any time of the year. Serve it with curries or egg dishes.

1 cup coarsely chopped dried apricots
1 cup coarsely chopped dried peaches
1 cup finely chopped pitted prunes
1 cup raisins
1 cup finely chopped onions
¾ cup malt vinegar
2 cups water, divided
½ cup packed brown sugar
2 garlic cloves, minced
2 teaspoons dry mustard
1½ teaspoons ground coriander
1 teaspoon grated orange peel
½ teaspoon ground cinnamon
½ teaspoon ground red pepper

In a deep 3-quart microwavable casserole, combine the apricots, peaches, prunes, raisins, onions, vinegar, 1½ cups of the water, sugar, garlic, mustard, coriander, orange peel, cinnamon, and red pepper. Cover with a lid or vented plastic wrap. Microwave on HIGH for 5 to 7 minutes, or until boiling; stir. Re-cover and microwave on MEDIUM for 20 minutes, stirring once during cooking. Stir in ½ cup of the water. Re-cover and microwave on MEDIUM for 10 to 15 minutes, or until the fruits are very soft; stir. Re-cover and let stand for 10 minutes. (If you prefer a looser chutney, add an additional ½ cup of water and microwave on MEDIUM for 4 to 6 minutes longer.)

Spoon into hot clean jars and cover tightly. Store in the refrigerator for 2 to 3 months.

Makes about 2 cups

SANTA ROSA PLUM PRESERVES

When I was working at Memorial Sloan Kettering Hospital in New York, Helen Lorant, a fellow manager, taught me home preserving. Here's what happened when my local market had an especially nice batch of Santa Rosa plums.

2 pounds Santa Rosa plums, pitted and coarsely chopped
1 pint fresh raspberries
½ cup water
1 cup sugar
2 tablespoons lemon juice
¼ teaspoon ground cinnamon

In a deep 3-quart microwavable casserole, combine the plums, raspberries, and water. Cover tightly with a lid or vented plastic wrap. Microwave on HIGH for 7 to 9 minutes, or until the plums are very tender. Let stand, covered, for 2 minutes. Uncover and cool slightly.

Using a slotted spoon, transfer the plum mixture to a food processor or blender; puree until the mixture is chunky; return to the casserole. Add the sugar, lemon juice, and cinnamon. Microwave on HIGH for 5 to 7 minutes, or until boiling. Stir until the sugar is completely dissolved. Microwave on HIGH for 12 to 18 minutes, or until the mixture has thickened, stirring several times during the cooking.

Spoon into hot clean jars and cover tightly. Store in the refrigerator for up to 6 weeks.

Makes about 2 cups

NOTE: These preserves are not canned or meant for long-term keeping. But they're so delicious, I doubt they'll be around for long.

PEACH-RASPBERRY JAM

Making jams and preserves from scratch is great fun and very rewarding. If you are at all timid, are certain they won't come out, or are convinced that preserving takes hours and hours, relax. Jel'n Jam is an all-in-one sugar and pectin mix. It's a terrific confidence-builder and a perfect way to get started.

2 pounds ripe peaches, peeled, pitted, and quartered
½ pint fresh raspberries
Grated peel of 1 lemon, yellow part only
Juice of 1 lemon
1 box of Kerr Jel'n Jam (32-ounce package)

Place the peaches in the workbowl of a food processor; pulse once or twice to barely crush the peaches. Add the raspberries; pulse several times until the raspberries are crushed and some small chunks of peaches remain.

Transfer the mixture to a deep 5-quart microwavable casserole. Stir in the lemon peel, lemon juice, and Jel'n Jam, mixing well until thoroughly combined. Microwave on HIGH for 15 to 20 minutes, or until the mixture comes to a full rolling boil, stirring every 5 minutes. Once the mixture comes to a full boil, cook for 5 minutes longer on HIGH. Skim foam from the top.

Ladle the jam into hot, clean jars and cover tightly. Cool to room temperature. Store in the refrigerator or freezer for 2 to 3 months.

Makes about 5 cups

AUTUMN HARVEST FRUIT SPREAD

There's no added sugar here, just the wholesome sweetness of prunes and raisins, in contrast to the tartness of apples and cranberries. I sometimes cook the fruits and don't puree them, making a delectable fruit relish.

1½ cups coarsely chopped pitted prunes
1½ cups golden raisins
1 large Granny Smith apple, peeled, cored, and coarsely chopped (about 8 ounces)
2 cups fresh or frozen cranberries
1½ cups unsweetened apple juice
⅓ cup chopped crystallized ginger
1 teaspoon lemon juice
¼ teaspoon almond extract

In a deep 3-quart microwavable casserole, combine the prunes, raisins, apple, cranberries, apple juice, and ginger. Cover tightly with a lid or vented plastic wrap. Microwave on HIGH for 10 to 12 minutes, or until boiling; stir. Re-cover and microwave for 4 to 6 minutes longer, or until the mixture has thickened. Stir in the lemon juice and almond extract. Cool slightly.

Puree the mixture in a food processor or blender. Spoon into hot clean jars and cover tightly. Store in the refrigerator or freezer for 2 to 3 months.

Makes 4 cups

YOGURT

Practically a staple item for most vegetarians, yogurt has been steadily gaining popularity with nonvegetarians too. Read the recipe through before starting and be sure to note that it takes several hours. You will need a microwave thermometer or temperature probe to check the yogurt along the way. The final result is a creamy, delicious, and very low-fat yogurt with fewer than ninety-five calories per cup. And—should you need any extra encouragement—there are no fillers, gums, or gelatins as are found in commercial varieties.

2½ cups nonfat dry milk powder
3½ cups water
⅓ cup plain yogurt

In a 2-quart microwavable casserole, slowly whisk together dry milk and water. Microwave on HIGH for 6 to 10 minutes, or until the temperature reaches 190°F., stirring once during cooking. Let the mixture cool to 115°F.

Stir about ½ cup of the mixture into the yogurt and return this to the milk, stirring constantly. Cover tightly with plastic wrap pulled taut across the casserole. Insert a thermometer or probe through the plastic, directly in the center. (If you get a good seal with the wrap, you should be able to lean the thermometer on the edge of the hole so that it stands completely straight. If you can't get the thermometer to stand, just place it through the opening when checking the temperature.)

When the temperature drops below 115°F., microwave on MEDIUM-LOW for 30 seconds to 1½ minutes, or until the temperature returns to 115°F. Let the mixture stand, covered, in the oven for the next 3 to 4 hours, (I find the time will vary depending on the weather, temperature in the kitchen, etc.)

Check the temperature every 20 to 25 minutes. If it drops below 110°F., microwave on MEDIUM-LOW for 45 to 75 seconds, or until the temperature returns to 115°F. Gently rotate the casserole 2 or 3 times during the process. Toward the end of the time you will see the mixture beginning to set when the casserole is lightly jiggled. The yogurt may need 1 or 2 more heatings. It is done when it appears set and you can see the indentation when the thermometer or probe is removed. Let stand, covered, for 15 minutes.

Quickly and carefully remove the plastic wrap to prevent water vapor from dripping back into the yogurt. Re-cover with a lid or tight plastic wrap. Refrigerate several hours or overnight, and the yogurt will set even more. The yogurt keeps in the refrigerator for 7 to 10 days.

Makes 4 cups

SAVORY OAT BRAN TOPPING

Substitute any combination of dried herbs and spices here. Store the blend in an airtight container so it's always ready to go. Use it on casseroles, baked macaroni, and vegetables.

1 cup oat bran
2 teaspoons dried thyme, crumbled
3 teaspoons garlic powder
½ teaspoon salt
½ teaspoon crushed red pepper

Place the bran in a 1-quart microwavable casserole. Microwave on HIGH for 2 to 4 minutes, stirring once. Add the remaining ingredients. Cool. Store in a cool, dry place, in a jar or tightly covered container.

Makes 1 cup

ITALIAN RICE BRAN TOPPING

Sprinkle this zesty high-fiber blend on pasta, pizza, or soup.

1 cup rice bran
¼ cup grated Parmesan cheese
1 teaspoon dried basil
½ teaspoon dried oregano, crumbled
½ teaspoon garlic powder
½ teaspoon ground black pepper

Place the rice bran in a 1-quart microwavable casserole. Microwave on HIGH for 2 to 4 minutes, stirring once. Cool. Stir in the remaining ingredients. Store in the refrigerator in a jar or tightly covered container.

••

Makes 1¼ cups

N O T E : Rice bran has a mild and nutty flavor. Be sure it is fresh when you purchase it by checking the date on the box. Otherwise, it will be dark colored and slightly bitter tasting.

SPICY SESAME SEED TOPPER

Just about any kind of seed—sunflower, pumpkin, as well as sesame—will provide a nice crunch in this topping. Toasting the seeds gives the mixture a richer flavor. Use this on biscuits or in a cold pasta salad.

••

1 cup sesame seeds
1 tablespoon vegetable oil
½ teaspoon curry powder
½ teaspoon garlic powder
¼ teaspoon salt

••

In a 1-quart microwavable casserole, combine the sesame seeds and oil. Stir in the curry powder, galic powder, and salt. Microwave on HIGH for 3 to 5 minutes, or until the seeds are golden, stirring twice during cooking. Cool. Store in the refrigerator in a jar or tightly covered container.

Makes 1 cup

••

COCOA-NUT TOPPING

This sweetened topping makes a nice addition to cereal or yogurt and can be sprinkled on top of muffins and sweet breads before baking. Include any of your favorite nuts.

1 cup wheat germ
¼ cup chopped walnuts
¼ cup packed brown sugar
1 tablespoon unsweetened cocoa
½ teaspoon ground cinnamon

Place the wheat germ and walnuts in a 1-quart microwavable casserole. Microwave on HIGH for 2 to 3 minutes, or until the nuts are lightly toasted, stirring once during cooking. Stir in the sugar, cocoa, and cinnamon. Cool. Store in the refrigerator in a jar or tightly covered container.

Makes about 1½ cups

COCOA CRUNCH TOPPING

¼ cup chopped nuts (optional)
3 tablespoons packed brown sugar
2 tablespoons Hershey's cocoa
2 tablespoons unbleached white flour
1 tablespoon margarine, softened

In small bowl combine, all the ingredients until crumbly.

Makes about ½ cup.

GREEN CURRY PASTE

If you're a fan of Thai curry—and the one on pages 118–119 is a good one to try—but are concerned about the shrimp paste that's usually included, worry no more. Barbara Hansen was kind enough to contribute this recipe from her book, *Taste of Southeast Asia*. Her traditional broiler method for the chilies gives a heartier, roasted flavor to the paste. But they can also be cooked in a microwave-safe plastic bag on HIGH for 2 to 3 minutes. You may also use well-rinsed canned chilies (not the pickled type).

2 large green Anaheim-type chilies
3 jalapeño peppers
2 large stalks cilantro, including roots, coarsely chopped (about 1 tablespoon)
3 tablespoons finely sliced lemon grass, 1 stalk (see Note)
4 shallots, coarsely chopped
4 large garlic cloves
1 teaspoon black peppercorns
1 teaspoon ground laos (see Note)
½ teaspoon ground cumin
½ teaspoon ground turmeric
¾ teaspoon salt
1 tablespoon vegetable oil

Preheat the broiler. Place the chilies on a baking sheet; roast under the broiler until blistered all over. Place in a paper bag for 15 minutes to steam. Peel. Discard stems and seeds.

Combine the peppers, cilantro, lemon grass, shallots, garlic, peppercorns, laos, cumin, turmeric, and salt in a blender or food processor fitted with the metal blade. Process as fine as possible. Pour into a small bowl and stir in the oil.

Cover and refrigerate at least 1 day before using to allow the flavors to blend. Refrigerate up to 1 week. Freeze for longer storage.

Makes ¾ cup

NOTE: This is available at Asian food markets.

HI-FI CRUNCH

Rolled oats, rice bran, and sunflower seeds are the high-fiber trio in this mildly sweetened, crunchy mixture. Sprinkle it into yogurt or applesauce or nibble it as a snack. Two tablespoons has about sixty-eight calories, almost two grams of protein, and no cholesterol.

1 cup rolled oats
½ cup rice bran
¼ cup sunflower seeds
1 tablespoon ground cinnamon
¼ cup dark maple syrup
1 tablespoon vegetable oil

In a 11 × 7-inch microwavable baking dish, combine the oats, rice bran, sunflower seeds, and cinnamon.

Pour maple syrup and oil over the top and stir until well combined. Gently shake the casserole or use the back of a spoon to make an even layer. Microwave on HIGH for 4 to 6 minutes, or until lightly toasted, stirring every 2 minutes. Be careful not to overcook. Let cool.

Store in the refrigerator in an airtight container for about 1 month.

Makes 2 cups

GARAM MASALA

Used in dal and other Indian dishes, garam masala is a blend of aromatic spices. Though it is traditionally roasted, this recipe will give you a simple and satisfactory substitute. Use this blend for Indian Dal (pages 106–107) or in soups, bean dishes, or casseroles where Indian flavors are desirable.

1 teaspoon ground cardamom
1 teaspoon ground cinnamon

1 teaspoon ground cloves
1 teaspoon ground coriander
1 teaspoon ground cumin
1 teaspoon ground ginger
1 teaspoon freshly ground black pepper

· ·

In a small bowl, combine all the ingredients. Store in a cool, dry place in an airtight container.

Makes about 2½ tablespoons

MULTIGRAIN MIX

Make your own grain mix and enjoy different tastes and textures in the same dish. Keep the mix in an airtight container in a cool, dry place and use it for a breakfast cereal, luncheon salad, or dinner entree, wherever you might use a single grain, such as rice. It adds new flavor and eye appeal to everyday dishes. I often add it to soups and pilafs for a change of pace.

· ·

1½ cups long-grain brown rice
1½ cups Wehani rice (see Note)
1 cup millet
1 cup pearl barley

· ·

Mix the brown and Wehani® rice, millet, and barley together. Pour into an airtight container. Store in a cool, dry place for 2 to 3 months.

Makes 5 cups

NOTE: Wehani rice is a rust-colored, aromatic brown rice sold in health-food stores. It is usually packaged by Lundberg Farms. Substitute regular basmati, white, or additional brown rice for the Wehani if you prefer. And by all means create mixes of your own using bulgur, oat groats, buckwheat, or whole-grain rye.

· ·

MENUS

SPINACH FOR LUNCH

Spinach Melt (pages 65–66)
Tossed Salad
Fresh Strawberries
Iced Tea

QUICK TO FIX DINNER

Main Meal-stuffed Potatoes (page 136)
Snow Peas and Carrots (page 156)
Seven-Grain Bread
Orange Sherbet

EGGS IN THE EVENING

Puffy Omelet (page 75)
Mustard Sauce (page 210)
Greek Spinach Rice (page 165)
Whole Wheat Toast
Fresh Fruit Compote (page 173)

INDIAN VEGETARIAN

Indian Dal (pages 106–107)
Basmati Rice Pilaf (page 166)
Steamed Spinach
Warmed Pita Breads
Fresh Mangoes

ITALIAN DELIGHT

Caponata (pages 40–41)
Lasagne Florentine Rolls (pages 96–97)
Caesar Salad
Poached Pears with Red Wine and Cassis (pages 174–175)

DINNER FOR FOUR

Stuffed Peppers (pages 133–134)
Spicy Corn Bread (page 68)
Steamed Broccoli
Fresh Pineapple Wedges

THANKSGIVING FEAST

Chestnut Soup (page 49)
Squash and Apple Bake (pages 147–148)
Baked Yams
Mushroom Rice Pilaf
Spicy Brussels Sprouts (page 155)
Hattie's Cranberry Sauce (page 213)
Angel Food Cake
Pumpkin Cheesecake Pie (pages 185–186)
Pecan Pie

FALL FOLIAGE BRUNCH

Cheddar-Jack Soup (page 50)
Three-Bread Stuffing (pages 134–135)
Cinnamon-scented Kabocha Squash (page 146)
Red–Leaf Lettuce Salad
Oatmeal Raisin Cookies

SUPER BOWL SUNDAY

Nachos Supreme (page 45)
Cheese Popcorn
Vegetarian Chili (pages 105–106)
Hot Cooked Rice (page 260)
Cocoa Brownies (pages 179–180)

MEXICAN FIESTA

Quesadillas with Salsa Verde (page 46)

Cheese Enchiladas (pages 140–141)
Red Rice
Pineapple Upside-down Cake

SUNDAY BRUNCH

Zucchini-Corn Strata (pages 139–140)
R. J.'s Roasted Potatoes (page 168)
Boston Lettuce with Spicy Honey Dressing
Rhubarb-Pear Crisp (pages 180–181)
Morning Zinger (page 91)

BREAKFAST BUFFET

Company Cocoa (page 90)
Banana–Date Bran Muffins (pages 86–87)
Fresh Pear Muffins (pages 88–89)
Zucchini-Apple Butter (page 218)
Santa Rosa Plum Preserves (page 220)
Apricot-Orange–Double Oat Cereal (pages 80–81)
Mixed Dried Fruits

COCKTAIL PARTY

Chilled Vegetable Platter (page 43)
Sushi (pages 122–125)
Scallion Bows with Mustard Sauce (page 44)
Cumin-roasted Cashews (page 42)
Assorted Cheeses
Champagne and Sparkling Mineral Water

OUTDOOR DINNER

Ratatouille (pages 128–129)
Apple Curry Rice (page 164)
Dilled Green Bean and Red Radish Salad (page 158)
Garlic Bread (page 66)
Lemon-Lime Sherbet
Golden Pound Cake

SPICY SUPPER

Carrot Soup (page 47)
Cauliflower Stew (page 130)
Rice Pilaf
Dried Fruit Chutney (page 219)
Almond Wafers

TASTE OF THAILAND

Thai Vegetable Curry (pages 118–119)
Brown Rice (page 260)
Spinach and Orange Salad
Sliced Bananas and Papayas
Hot Ginger Tea

PEANUT BUTTER BREAKFAST

Glazed Grapefruit (page 83)
Peanut Butter on Raisin Toast
Raspberry Tea

SUMMER PASTA PARTY

Linguine with Fresh Vegetables and Herbs (pages 98–99)
Tomato and Basil Salad
Sesame Breadsticks
Summer Fruit Tart (pages 184–185)

BREAKFAST ON THE RUN

Cranberry-Orange Pleaser (page 92)
Breakfast Burrito (page 81)

SPANISH VEGETARIAN

Chilled Gazpacho
Vegetarian Paella (pages 125–126)
Mixed Green Salad
Fresh Peaches with Gingered Cream

PREPARED IN ADVANCE DINNER

Stuffed Eggplant (pages 138–139)
Herbed Green and Yellow Squash (page 145)
Sourdough Rolls
Fresh Melon and Berries

QUICK AND EASY SUPPER

Chilled Roasted Peppers
Risotto with Asparagus, Mushrooms, and Fontina (pages 112–113)
Arugula Salad
Italian Whole Wheat Bread
Fresh Figs and Nectarines

EASY AUTUMN DINNER

Esther's Leek and Potato Soup (page 48)
Stuffed Chayote (pages 132–133)
Dilled Green Beans
Sweet Potato–Apple Cake (pages 178–179)

QUICK SNACKS

Fresh Fruit Compote (page 173)
Plain Yogurt

Baked Pears (page 175) and Gingersnap Cookies

Wisconsin Cheddar Cheese,
Whole Wheat Crackers, and Applesauce (page 176)

CHECKLIST FOR HEALTHY EATING

HOW MICROWAVE OVENS FIT INTO VEGETARIAN COOKING

If you skipped over the introduction, you may have missed the point of how well suited vegetables are for microwave cooking. Their color is beautifully maintained and their flavor is intensified because they are cooked so quickly and with so little water. The real bonus is in the superior nutrient retention of foods that are cooked in the microwave oven.

This is especially true of the B vitamins and vitamin C, which are water-soluble. They are also a bit fragile and can break down on exposure to high heat. Because microwave cooking is so fast and cooking vegetables this way requires but a few tablespoons of water, the cooking time is much shorter. All in all, this means better nutrient retention.

WHAT IT MEANS TO BE A VEGETARIAN

The reasons for choosing a vegetarian lifestyle are varied. For many it is part of the religious or cultural environment in which they were raised. Others have chosen to be vegetarians because of the ecological implications of eating lower on the food chain. These people feel that consuming plant protein presents less of a demand on the world's food supply and may help to alleviate world hunger problems. There are also strong economic considerations since meals low in animal protein are generally less expensive than those that are meat-based. The issue of animal rights and ethical issues prompt others to reduce or eliminate the consumption of meat.

Yet when people boast to me about being vegetarians and then go on to relate all the foods they have eliminated from their diets, panic is usually my first reaction. Without guidance and proper planning, an extreme approach can lead to nutritional deficiencies. When eliminating or reducing animal products in the diet, it is necessary to make some nutrient compensations to avoid becoming anemic or malnourished.

It's important to realize that good eating takes good planning and good information, regardless of your preferences. With a clear purpose everyone can maintain or build good health. Some very basic information will get you started and keep you on the road to success.

Try to set a few goals and objectives for yourself if you are not already a vegetarian and wish to become one. For instance, do you just want to include more whole grains in your diet, or reduce to some degree the amount of meat you consume, or totally revamp the way you eat? Keep these goals written down, not just in your mind.

SOME HEALTH CONSIDERATIONS

More and more evidence indicates that consuming less meat and fat and adding more cereals, grains, fruits, and vegetables to your diet can alleviate a number of health problems. There is also speculation that these dietary changes may prevent the occurrence of such problems in the first place. If you are already a vegetarian, commit to being the best and healthiest one you can be, and perhaps use this time to reevaluate how you're doing and where you stand.

One bonus that many people find when they become vegetarians is that they lose weight in the transition or that their personal best weight is easier to maintain. Studies indicate that vegetarians have weights that are closer to desirable levels than nonvegetarians. This is probably due to the fact that vegetables, grains, and fruits are high in bulk (fiber) and are good "satiety" foods. This means that they are satisfying and that it feels as if you are eating more, even though the calories may actually be fewer than you would normally consume—provided that the foods are not loaded with fat and excess sugar.

But don't get me wrong, there are plenty of overweight vegetarians out there too! I think it's part of the "if a little is good, a lot is better" syndrome that puts these people over the line. What often happens is that people stop using butter and start using lots of vegetable oil or stop using white sugar and put honey on everything.

All foods have calories. The quickest and easiest summary I can give you, regardless of your preferences, are the guidelines of The American Dietetic Association: variety and moderation. Once you learn and practice these, your life will be much less complicated and your nutritional status will, in most cases, take care of itself.

In 1989, the National Research Council, an arm of the National Academy of Sciences, issued a revised set of Dietary Guidelines for Americans. This report was the most comprehensive report on diet and health ever published. The recommendations were prepared by nineteen diet and health experts with the hope of resolving some dietary issues for consumers. Briefly, their recommendations were as follows:

- Eat five or more half-cup servings of fruits and vegetables daily, including citrus fruits and green and yellow vegetables.

- Increase bread, cereal, and other starch consumption to six or more servings per day, so that carbohydrates are more than 55 percent of total calories.

- Consume moderate amounts of protein (about six ounces of meat or its equivalent) per day.

- Reduce fat consumption to 30 percent of total calories per day. Cut saturated fat to 10 percent or less and reduce cholesterol to a maximum of 300 milligrams daily.

In addition to these simple and straightforward guidelines, there are some other specific nutrition considerations for vegetarians that deserve special attention. Keep these in mind when planning daily menus so that your nutritional intake is always adequate.

1. Protein is a prime consideration. Protein is the building block of life, and for the most part, is not stored in the body the way carbohydrates and fats are. Composed of amino acids, proteins enter the body through the foods we eat. The proteins are broken down; the amino acids are reshuffled and recombined to make new proteins for whatever function they might be needed.

When proteins from grains, legumes, seeds, nuts, and vegetables are mixed, the amino acid profiles are supplemented so that deficits in one are made up by another. This mixing is the concept of mutual supplementation or protein complementation. At one time this was a major point for vegetarians and the idea of having certain foods, such as rice and beans, at the same meal so that a full protein was supplied was stressed. Though this is sometimes tasty and convenient, it is not mandatory.

The position of The American Dietetic Association in a technical support paper on vegetarian diets is clearly states that: "Intakes of different types of protein that complement one another should be eaten over the course of the day." The paper goes on to say that "it is not necessary that complementation of amino acid profiles be precise and at exactly the same meal."

It's also good to remember that whenever an animal protein, such as an egg or a small amount of milk or cheese, is added to a plant protein, the overall protein value of that plant is enhanced. When a varied diet is consumed on a daily basis, adequate amounts of amino acids can be obtained from a plant-based diet.

You may be curious about what plants can be substituted for meat. Some exchanges you may want to keep in mind that can usually be substituted for for protein in 1 ounce of meat are:

- 4 ounces of tofu

- 3 egg whites

- 1 whole egg

- 1 tablespoon of peanut butter

- 1 cup of cooked beans (legumes)

- 1 ounce of cheese, such as Cheddar, Monterey Jack, or Swiss

- ¼ cup of cottage cheese

2. Iron from meat protein, also known as *heme* iron, is better absorbed than the iron from plant foods, *non heme* iron. Dietary fiber, tannin, like that found in tea and red wine, as well as diets that are high in soy protein, can reduce the absorption of iron. On the other hand, iron absorption can be boosted by including foods high in vitamin C in the diet. It is certainly easy enough to drink a glass of tomato or orange juice with meals. Another solution is to look for recipes that include sources of both iron and vitamin C. For instance, prepare iron-rich foods such as tofu, brown rice, and lentils with a sauce or salad made with peppers, tomatoes, or other vitamin C sources. One report states that the vitamin C in fruits and vegetables can triple iron absorption from other foods eaten at the same meal.

Good plant sources of iron include kale, spinach, and dandelion greens. Prune juice, cooked prunes, raisins, and figs, as well as almonds, cashews, filberts, and pecans will help boost the iron content of meals and snacks.

You will want to keep in mind that compounds known as phytates and oxalates are naturally occurring in many plant foods, especially wheat and dark green vegetables. The action of these compounds is to bind certain minerals and make them unavailable for utilization and absorption in the body. So do not rely on plants and whole grains as exclusive sources of minerals like iron and calcium, because you may not be getting the full mineral value. Once again, variety and moderation are your best guidelines.

3. Calcium deserves special attention here. Most lacto-ovo-vegetarians (those who consume eggs and dairy products) have a sufficient amount of calcium in their diets. A beneficial effect for these people is that they reportedly have greater bone density and a decreased risk for osteoporosis than nonvegetarians. Diets of vegans (those who consume only vegetables, fruits, and nuts), however, contain a limited supply of calcium. Because of their avoidance of eggs and dairy products, they may have a problem obtaining adequate amounts of calcium from the foods they eat. Calcium is one of the minerals that can also be bound by fiber, and so, the problem for them may be compounded. There are some steps to take to augment calcium utilization. Milk and milk products are an obvious source of calcium, but so is dry milk and it can be a nonfat product. Add it to casseroles, soups, stews, and desserts. Though it was not mentioned specifically in the National Research Council's Dietary Guidelines, adults should consume at least two servings of milk and children, three to four.

Dark green leafy vegetables, such as chard, collards, and broccoli as well as sea vegetables, such as kelp, nori, and hiziki, can provide a good supply of calcium. Check package labels for foods such as calcium-fortified whole wheat bread, corn tortillas, and tofu that provide high levels of calcium. These items can be utilized by the body in much the same way as dairy products. Those to look for are tofu prepared with calcium-sulfate rather than nigari, and tortillas that are made from lime-treated corn rather than flour tortillas.

4. Zinc, too, may present a difficulty for vegetarians. Though the best source of zinc are meat, poultry, and seafood, it is widespread in plant foods. Again, fiber and phytates can hinder availability. Zinc may have greater nutritional importance than was once thought and is currently under investigation both for vegetarians and the general population. In the meantime, it might be wise to eat a varied diet. Legumes, nuts, seeds, nutritional yeast, and hard cheeses are foods in which zinc can be found.

5. Vitamin B-12 is not found in plant foods; it can be derived only from animal sources. The requirement for vitamin B-12 is minute. It is a very important nutrient.

The body is able to store vitamin B-12—about four years' worth—so it takes a long time for a deficiency to develop after a person gives up eating animal products. When it does occur, however, it can cause irreversible damage to the brain and nerves.

Fortunately, vitamin B-12 can be isolated, stabilized, and used alone as a supplement or to fortify foods. Such foods are so labeled, but the labels may be misleading. The average vegetarian is probably getting an adequate supply of vitamin B-12 from milk and milk products. Vegans, however, should supplement their diets with a source of vitamin B-12, such as a cobalamin tablet. A properly fortified soy milk or breakfast cereal can also ensure an adequate intake of vitamin B-12.

GROUPS WITH SPECIAL NEEDS

My training as a registered dietitian has made me very aware that the elderly, young children, pregnant or breast-feeding women, or those recovering from an illness have special nutrient needs. As a nutritionist I also know that well-planned vegetarian diets can be adequate for everyone. When there is a special situation or if a clinical condition exists (diabetes, for instance), professional assistance may be in order. In those cases, such as pregnancy, supplements and specially fortified foods will be needed to ensure adequacy. Anyone in the groups mentioned above or those who wish to change their current eating habits should be particular about getting sound and competent advice from a qualified nutrition specialist. They will find it helpful to consult a registered dietitian who can help them plan menus that will meet their unique nutritional demands.

STRATEGIES FOR SUCCESS

Selecting foods wisely should be your main goal. To achieve that goal, take a look at the chart that follows. It will offer you a quick reference guide for choosing foods. Remember that there are no magical combinations or times of the day to eat certain foods. Plan to choose a wide variety of foods from food each of the groups.

A way to do that is to keep lots of colors and textures in the food choices that you make throughout the day. Not only does it make eating more visually appealing, but it usually indicates that you are choosing greater variety from each of the food groups. Chances are that you will also be consuming a greater variety of nutrients. Go beyond green leafy vegetables by also selecting reds, oranges, and yellows in vegetables like tomatoes, peppers, carrots, squash, and corn. The same goes for fruits, where mangoes, kiwis, and cantaloupes can be added to pears, apples, and oranges. Cereals, grains, milk, yogurt, beans, nuts, steamed vegetables, and raw and cooked fruits all offer a variety of textures, as well as a good mix from each of the food groups.

FOOD GROUP	DAILY SERVINGS	SERVING SIZE
Protein	4–6 ounces	4 ounces tofu 1 cup cooked beans ¼ cup cottage cheese 1 egg
Cereals, grains, and breads	6–11	1 slice bread 1 tortilla (6-inch) ½ pita bread (6-inch) ½ cup cooked rice, pasta, or cereal
Dairy Products	2 (adults) 3–4 (children)	1 cup milk 1 cup yogurt 1⅓ cups cottage cheese

(continued)

FOOD GROUP	DAILY SERVINGS	SERVING SIZE
Vegetables and fruits	5	
Vitamin A (dark green leafy and deep yellow vegetables)	2	½ cup cooked or 1 cup raw vegetable or ½ cup juice or 1 medium fruit: spinach, collards, sweet potato, pumpkin, carrots, winter squash; mango, cantaloupe, papaya
Vitamin C (increases iron absorption)	3	½ cup cooked or 1 cup raw vegetable or ½ cup juice or 1 medium fruit: broccoli, Brussels sprouts, cabbage, cauliflower, green and red peppers; citrus fruits, cantaloupe, strawberries, tomatoes
Fats and oils	2	1 tablespoon vegetable oil: canola, corn, olive, peanut, safflower, soy, etc.; mayonnaise, salad dressing
Potatoes, other vegetables and fruits	2	1 medium potato or ½ cup cooked or 1 cup raw vegetable or 1 medium fruit, or ½ cup juice: corn, green beans, beets, green peas, summer squash; apples, pears, plums, bananas, grapes, cherries

MASTER SECRETS

The point of the Master Secrets chapter is to provide you with a quick reference for selecting fruits and vegetables when they are in season and at their peak of flavor.

Following that is a chart for preparing a number of vegetables and grains. At a glance you can see how much to prepare, the essential ingredients, appropriate cookware, cooking time, and standing time.

When you're cooking—and especially when you're in a rush— there are many times when it would be much easier to have things on hand like cooked rice to make salads, soups, or desserts. Creating or altering a recipe becomes second nature when the basic ingredients are ready and waiting. It's always nice to have some chilled asparagus, cooked carrots, or fruit compote to help make a quick meal or snack.

If you're a weekend chef, you know that weekends are a good time to cook ahead. Making up a few batches of your personal favorites means express meals for the rest of the week.

FRUIT AND VEGETABLE AVAILABILITY GUIDE

KEY
- • = **Regular Availability**
- + = **Peak Season**

	JAN.	FEB.	MARCH	APRIL	MAY	JUNE	JULY	AUG.	SEPT.	OCT.	NOV.	DEC.
FRUITS												
Apples	+	+	+	+	+	•	•	•	+	+	+	+
Apricots	•			•	+	•	•					•
Avocados	•	+	+	+	+	+	+	+	•	•	•	•
Bananas	•	•	•	•	•	•	•	•	•	•	•	•

(continued)

Fruits *(continued)*

	JAN.	FEB.	MARCH	APRIL	MAY	JUNE	JULY	AUG.	SEPT.	OCT.	NOV.	DEC.
Blueberries					•	•	+	+	+	•		
Cantaloupe	•	•	•		+	+	+	+	•	•	•	•
Cherries	•	•		•	•	+	+	•				•
Grapefruit	+	+	+	•	•	•	•	•	•	•	•	+
Grapes	•	•	•	•	+	+	+	+	+	+	+	+
Honeydew	•	•	•	+	+	+	+	+	•	•	•	•
Kiwi	+	•	•	•	•	+	+	•	•	•	•	+
Lemons	•	•	•		+	+	+	+	•	•	+	+
Limes	+	•	•	•	•	+	+	+	+	•	+	+
Melons	•	•		•	+	+	+	+	+	•	•	•
Nectarines	+	+	•	•	•	+	+	+	•	•	•	•
Oranges	•	+	+	+	•	•	•	•	•	•	+	+
Papaya	•	•	•		+	+	+	+	+	•		
Peaches	+	+	•	•	•	+	+	+	•	•	•	•
Pears	•	•	•	•	•			•	•	•	•	•
Pineapple	+	+	+	+	+	+	+	+	+	•	•	+
Plums	+	+	•	•	•	+	+	+	+	+	+	+
Raspberries/ Blackberries		•	•	•		•	•	•	•			
Strawberries	•	•	+	+	+	•	•	•	•	•	+	•
Tangerines	•	•	•	•	•					•	•	•
Tomatoes	+	+	+	+	+	•	+	+	+	+	•	+
Watermelon	•	•	+	+	+	+	+	+	•	•	•	•

	JAN.	FEB.	MARCH	APRIL	MAY	JUNE	JULY	AUG.	SEPT.	OCT.	NOV.	DEC.
VEGETABLES												
Artichokes	•	+	+	+	•	•	•	•	•	•	•	•
Asparagus	+	+	+	+	+	•		•	•	•	•	•
Beans/Snap	•	•	•	•	•	•	•	•	•	•	•	•
Beets	•	•	•	•	•	•	+	+	+	•	•	•
Broccoli	•	•	+	+	+	+	+	+	+	+	+	•
Brussels Sprouts	+	+	•	•	•	•	•	•	•	+	+	+
Cabbage	+	+	+	+	+	+	•	+	+	+	+	+
Carrots	•	•	•	•	•	•	+	+	+	+	+	+
Cauliflower	+	+	•	+	+	+	+	+	+	+	+	+
Celery	•	•	•	•	•	•	•	•	•	•	•	•
Corn	+	+	+	+	+	+	+	+	•	•	•	+
Cucumber	+	+	•	+	+	•	+	+	•	•	•	•
Eggplant	+	+	+	+	+	+	+	+	+	+	•	•
Endive/Escarole	•	•	+	+	+	•	•	•	•	•	•	•
Garlic	•	•	•	•	•	•	•	•	•	•	•	•
Ginger	•	•	•	•	•	•	•	•	•	•	•	•
Herbs, Fresh	•	•	•	•	•	•	•	•	•	•	•	•
Horseradish Root	•	•	+	+	+	•	•	•	•	•	•	•
Kale	+	+	•	•	•	•	•	•	•	•	•	+
Leeks	+	+	+	+	•	•	•	•	•	+	+	+
Lettuce, Boston Bibb	+	+	+	+	•	•	+	+	+	•	•	•

(continued)

	JAN.	FEB.	MARCH	APRIL	MAY	JUNE	JULY	AUG.	SEPT.	OCT.	NOV.	DEC.
Lettuce, Iceberg	+	+	+	+	+	+	+	+	+	+	•	+
Lettuce, Leaf	•	•	•	•	•	•	+	+	+	•	•	•
Mushrooms	•	•	•	•	•	•	•	•	•	•	•	•
Onions, Dry	+	+	+	+	+	+	+	•	+	+	+	+
Onions, Green	+	+	+	+	+	+	+	+	•	•	+	+
Peas, Green	+	+	+	+	+	+	+	•	•	•	•	•
Peppers, Sweet	+	+	•	+	+	•	•	•	+	+	+	•
Potatoes	•	•	•	•	•	•	•	•	•	•	•	•
Radishes	•	+	+	+	+	•	•	•	•	•	•	•
Romaine	•	•	•	•	•	•	•	+	+	+	•	•
Spinach	+	+	•	•	•	+	+	+	•	•	•	•
Sprouts	•	•	•	•	•	•	•	•	•	•	•	•
Squash, Summer	•	•	•	•	•	+	+	+	•	•	•	•
Squash, Winter	•	•	•	•	•	•	•	•	•	•	•	•
Sweet Potatoes	•	•	•	•	•	•	•	•	•	•	+	+
Baby Carrots	•	•	•	•	•	•	•	•	•	•	•	•
Baby Corn	•	•	•	•	•	+	+	+	•	•	•	•
Baby Eggplant	•	•	•	•	•	+	+	+	•	•	•	•
Baby Lettuce	•	•	•	•	•	•	•	•	•	•	•	•
Baby Squash	•	•	•	•	•	+	+	+	•	•	•	•

SPECIALTIES

	JAN.	FEB.	MARCH	APRIL	MAY	JUNE	JULY	AUG.	SEPT.	OCT.	NOV.	DEC.
Belgian Endive	+	+	+	+	•	•	•	•	•	•	+	+
Carambola	•	•	•						•	+	+	•

	JAN.	FEB.	MARCH	APRIL	MAY	JUNE	JULY	AUG.	SEPT.	OCT.	NOV.	DEC.
Exotic Mushrooms	•	•	•	•	•	•	•	•	•	•	•	•
Jicama	+	•	•	•	+	+	+	•	•	•	+	+
Plantains	•	•	•	•	•	•	•	•	•	•	•	•
Radicchio	•	•	•	•	•	•	•	•	•	•	•	•
Shallots	•	•	•	•	•	•	•	•	•	•	•	•

Source: Compiled by Produce Marketing Association, 1500 Casho Mill Road, P.O. Box 6036, Newark, DE 19714-6036 (302 738-7100). Reprinted with permission.

CHART FOR VEGETABLES, GRAINS, AND CEREALS

VEGETABLES

All vegetables are covered and cooked at HIGH, unless otherwise indicated. Use shortest time first, then proceed. Let stand for suggested time. Adjust time if vegetables are larger or smaller than indicated here. These vegetables are cooked tender-crisp.

TYPE	AMOUNT	CONTAINER	PREPARATION	COOKING TIME	STANDING TIME COVERED
Artichokes	2 medium	9-inch pie plate	Remove outer leaves, snip tips; cut off stem. Add ½ cup water. Cover and pierce base with tip of sharp knife to test doneness.	7–10 minutes	5 minutes
Asparagus (medium width stalks)	1 pound	12-inch round plate	Wash, snap off tough bases. Arrange asparagus so that tips are toward center of dish. Sprinkle with 2 tablespoons water. Cover and vent. Rearrange once.	5–7 minutes	4 minutes
Beans (green and wax) Cut	1 pound	1½-quart casserole	Wash, drain, and cut into 1½-inch pieces. Add ¼ cup water. Cover and vent. Stir once.	6–10 minutes	5 minutes
Whole		1½-quart casserole	Wash and drain; add ¼ cup water. Cover and vent. Stir after first 4 minutes, then every 2 minutes thereafter until tender-crisp.	8–12 minutes	5 minutes
Beans broad, fava, and lima	2 cup	1½-quart casserole	Shell and rinse. Sprinkle with 3 tablespoons water. Cover and vent. Stir once.	12–14 minutes	3 minutes

TYPE	AMOUNT	CONTAINER	PREPARATION	COOKING TIME	STANDING TIME COVERED
Dried beans black, kidney, pinto, navy, Great Northern, chick peas	1 cup	3-quart casserole	Precook: Add 2 cups water. Cover tightly with lid and wrap or double wrap.	Precook: **High** 5–8 minutes, or to boiling. Stir. **Medium** 2 minutes	1 hour; drain
			Cook: Add 3 cups water. Cover tightly with lid and wrap or double wrap.	Cook: **High** 5–8 minutes, or to boiling. Stir. **Medium** 25–35 minutes, or until tender. Stir after 15 minutes	5 minutes
Dried beans broad, fava, lima	1 cup	3-quart casserole	Precook: Add 2 cups water. Cover tightly with lid and wrap or double wrap.	Precook: **High** 5–8 minutes, or to boiling. Stir. **Medium** 2 minutes	1 hour; drain
			Cook: Add 3 cups water. Cover tightly with lid and wrap or double wrap.	Cook: **High** 5–8 minutes, or to boiling. Stir. **Medium** 25 to 35 minutes, or until tender. Stir after 15 minutes	5 minutes
Beets	4 medium (about 1½ pounds)	1-quart casserole	Scrub and trim tops to 1 inch; leave root stem. Add ¼ cup water. Cover and vent. Stir once.	12–16 minutes	5 minutes

(continued)

TYPE	AMOUNT	CONTAINER	PREPARATION	COOKING TIME	STANDING TIME COVERED
Broccoli					
Cut	1 pound	2-quart casserole	Discard about 1 inch of tough stalk. Cut remainder into 1-inch pieces, leaving florets slightly longer. Wash. Sprinkle with 1 tablespoon water. Cover and vent. Stir once.	5–8 minutes	3 minutes
Spears	1 pound	2-quart rectangular dish	Cut into spears, leaving about 3 inches of stalk. Wash. Place buds toward center of dish. Sprinkle with 2 tablespoons water. Cover and vent.	7–10 minutes	4 minutes
Brussels sprouts	1 pound (medium)	1½-quart casserole	Trim stem; cut × in bottom. Wash; add ¼ cup water. Cover and vent. Stir once.	6–8 minutes	4 minutes
Cabbage (green or red) Shredded	1 pound	3-quart casserole	Add 2 tablespoons water. Cover and vent. Stir once.	4–6 minutes	3 minutes
Cabbage Napa	1½ pounds	3-quart casserole	Discard wilted leaves. Wash; cut lengthwise and slice in 1-inch pieces. Sprinkle with 2 tablespoons water. Cover and vent. Stir once.	5–7 minutes	3 minutes
Carrots Sliced	1 pound	1-quart casserole	Scrub or peel; cut into ¼-inch slices. Sprinkle with 2 tablespoons water. Cover and vent. Stir once.	6–7 minutes	4 minutes

TYPE	AMOUNT	CONTAINER	PREPARATION	COOKING TIME	STANDING TIME COVERED
Whole	1 pound	2-quart baking dish	Scrub or peel; trim ends. Add ¼ cup water. Cover and vent. Rearrange after half of time	9–11 minutes	3 minutes
Whole, baby	1 pound	1-quart casserole	Scrub or peel; trim ends. Sprinkle with 2 tablespoons water. Cover and vent. Stir once.	6–8 minutes	3 minutes
Cauliflower					
Florets	1½ pounds (1 head)	2-quart casserole	Trim, core, and break into florets. Add ¼ cup water. Cover and vent. Stir once.	5–7 minutes	3 minutes
Whole	1½ pounds (1 head)	2-quart casserole	Trim and core. Add ¼ cup water. Cover and vent.	8–11 minutes	5 minutes
Celeriac	1 pound (1 whole)	1-quart casserole	Pierce skin; scrub. Add ¼ cup water. Cover and vent.	7–9 minutes	3 minutes
Celery	2 cups (slices)	1-quart casserole	Add 3 tablespoons water. Cover and vent. Stir once.	3–5 minutes	2 minutes
Corn					
Cob	1 ear	—	Leave in husk or loosely wrap in paper or place in towel covered dish with 2 tablespoons water.	4–6 minutes	3 minutes
	4 ears	—	Same as above, using ¼ cup water. Turn twice.	9–12 minutes	5 minutes

(continued)

253

TYPE	AMOUNT	CONTAINER	PREPARATION	COOKING TIME	STANDING TIME COVERED
Kernels (fresh)	2 cups	1-quart casserole	Sprinkle with 2 tablespoons water. Cover and vent. Stir once.	4–6 minutes	2 minutes
Eggplant Whole, tender	1 pound	Oven floor	Pierce skin in several places. Lay on double layer of paper towels. Turn once.	6 minutes	1 minute
Whole, soft	1 pound	Oven floor	Same as above.	8–9 minutes	1 minute
Fennel	1½ pounds (2 bulbs)	9-inch square dish	Trim tops; cut in half lengthwise. Add ¼ cup water. Cover and vent. Turn once.	7–9 minutes	3 minutes
Greens collards, kale, mustard	2 pounds	3-quart casserole	Rinse but do not dry. Coarsely chop. Cover and vent. Stir once.	7–10 minutes	3 minutes
Jerusalem Artichokes (Sunchokes)	1 pound	2-quart casserole	Scrub or peel; cut into ¼-inch slices. Sprinkle with 2 tablespoons water. Cover and vent. Stir once.	5–8 minutes	4 minutes
Jicama	1 pound	2-quart casserole	Peel; cut into 1-inch cubes. Sprinkle with 3 tablespoons water. Cover and vent. Stir once.	6–9 minutes	3 minutes
Kohlrabi	4 medium (1 pound)	1-quart casserole	Cut off leaves and stems; scrub. Add 2 tablespoons water. Cover and vent. Stir once.	6–9 minutes	3 minutes

TYPE	AMOUNT	CONTAINER	PREPARATION	COOKING TIME	STANDING TIME COVERED
Leeks	1½ pounds	9-inch square dish	Trim roots and tops, leaving 1½-inch green part. Cut in half. Rinse thoroughly to remove sand. Sprinkle with 2 tablespoons water. Cover and vent. Rearrange once.	8–14 minutes	5 minutes
Mushrooms					
Sliced	1 pound	2-quart casserole	Sprinkle with 2 tablespoons water. Cover and vent. Stir once.	3–5 minutes	2 minutes
Whole	1 pound	2-quart casserole	Wash and trim stem. Same as above.	3½–6 minutes	2 minutes
Okra	1 pound	2-quart casserole	Trim stems without piercing pod. Wash but do not dry. Cover and vent. Stir once.	4–6 minutes	2 minutes
Onions					
Pearl	1 pound	1½-quart casserole	Peel; sprinkle with 2 tablespoons water. Cover and vent. Stir once.	5–7 minutes	5 minutes
Scallions	½ pound	2-quart baking dish	Trim; sprinkle with 2 tablespoons water. Cover and vent. Rearrange once.	3–5 minutes	3 minutes
White or yellow	1 pound	1½-quart casserole	Peel and cut into ¼-inch slices. Stir to separate. Sprinkle with 2 tablespoons water or oil. Cover and vent. Stir once.	6–8 minutes	3 minutes

(continued)

TYPE	AMOUNT	CONTAINER	PREPARATION	COOKING TIME	STANDING TIME COVERED
Parsnips	4 medium (1 pound)	1½-quart casserole	Scrub or peel. Cut into ½-inch pieces. Sprinkle with 2 tablespoons water. Cover and vent. Stir once.	4–6 minutes	3 minutes
Peas					
Green, shelled	2 cups	1½-quart casserole	Sprinkle with 2 tablespoons water. Cover and vent. Stir once.	4–6 minutes	2 minutes
Snow or Sugar Snap	1 pound	1½-quart casserole	Rinse, but do not dry. Cover and vent. Stir once.	5–7 minutes	3 minutes
Peas, split, or lentils	1 cup	3-quart casserole	Rinse, drain, and sort out any debris. Add 3 cups water. Cover tightly. Cook in two stages. Stir after boiling.	**High** 7 minutes, or until boiling. **Medium** 30 minutes, or until tender	10 minutes
Potatoes	8 ounces each	Oven floor	Scrub. Pierce skin with a fork or tip of sharp knife. Place on double layer of paper towels. Arrange 1 inch apart in a circle. Turn once during cooking. Wrap in paper or terry towel for standing time.		
	1 potato			4–6 minutes	5–10 minutes
	2 potatoes			6–8 minutes	
	3 potatoes			12–14 minutes	
	4 potatoes			15–20 minutes	

TYPE	AMOUNT	CONTAINER	PREPARATION	COOKING TIME	STANDING TIME COVERED
Rutabagas	1 pound	1½-quart casserole	See Turnips	10–12 minutes	3 minutes
Spinach	1 pound	3-quart casserole	Trim and rinse but do not dry. Cover and vent. Stir once.	4–6 minutes	2 minutes
Squash					
Acorn or Butternut	1 medium (1½ pounds)	2-quart baking dish	Cook whole. Pierce with fork or sharp knife. Cover and vent. Turn after 5 minutes.	8–10 minutes	5–8 minutes
Chayote	2 medium (¾ pound each)	11 x 7-inch baking dish	Cut in half; add 2 tablespoons water. Cover and vent. Turn after 3 minutes.	6–8 minutes	5 minutes
Spaghetti	3½ pounds	2-quart baking dish	Cook whole. Pierce skin or cut in half. Same as above. Turn after 5 minutes.	10–15 minutes	5 minutes
Summer	1 pound	1–quart casserole	Slice into ½-inch pieces; add 3 tablespoons water. Cover and vent. Stir once.	4–6 minutes	2 minutes
Sweet potatoes or yams	8 ounces each	Oven floor	Scrub. Pierce skin with a fork or tip of sharp knife. Place on double layer of paper towels. Arrange 1 inch apart in a circle. Turn once during cooking. Wrap in paper or terry towel for standing.		
	1 potato			4–5 minutes	5–10 minutes
	2 potatoes			6–7 minutes	

(continued)

Vegetables *(continued)*

TYPE	AMOUNT	CONTAINER	PREPARATION	COOKING TIME	STANDING TIME COVERED
Sweet potatoes or yams *(cont.)*	3 potatoes 4 potatoes			8–10 minutes 10–12 minutes	
Swiss chard	1½ pounds	3-quart casserole	Rinse and cut ribs into ½-inch pieces. Sprinkle with 1 tablespoon water. Cover and vent. Cut leaves into ½-inch strips. Stir in after 3 minutes. Cover and vent.	7–9 minutes	2 minutes
Turnips	1 pound	1½-quart casserole	Peel and cut into 1-inch chunks. Sprinkle with 2 tablespoons water. Cover and vent. Stir once.	6–9 minutes	3 minutes

Source: Compiled by the author.

*Liquid may be water, stock, or fruit juice.

**For 4 servings.

GRAINS

TYPE	AMOUNT	CONTAINER	PREPARATION	COOKING TIME	STANDING TIME COVERED
Barley					
Pearled	1 cup	3-quart casserole	Combine with 3 cups water and ½ teaspoon salt, if desired. Cover tightly. Cook until tender; drain. (Yield 3½ cups.)	**High** 4–6 minutes, or until boiling. **Medium-High** 30–40 minutes, or until tender.	None
Hulled	1 cup	3-quart casserole	Same as above. Use 3¼ cups water.	Add additional time until tender.	None
Bulgur (medium grain)	1 cup	1- to 2-quart casserole	Pour 2 cups boiling liquid* over bulgur. Cover tightly. Let stand 20 to 30 minutes or until water is absorbed. (Yield 3 cups.)	—	20–30 minutes
Couscous (instant)	1 cup	1-quart casserole	Combine with 1½ cups liquid* with 2 teaspoons oil and ½ teaspoon salt, if desired. Microwave on HIGH for 2 minutes or until boiling. Stir in couscous. Cover tightly. (Yields 3½ cups.)		5 minutes
Job's Tear	1 cup	1-quart casserole	Combine with 2 cups liquid* and a pinch of salt. Cover tightly. (Yield 3⅓ cups)	**High** 6–8 minutes, or to boiling. **Medium-Low** 45–55 minutes, or until tender.	10 minutes

(continued)

TYPE	AMOUNT	CONTAINER	PREPARATION	COOKING TIME	STANDING TIME COVERED
Quinoa	1 cup	1- to 2-quart casserole	Combine with 2 cups liquid* and ½ teaspoon salt, if desired. Cover tightly.	**High** 4–6 minutes, or to boiling. **Medium** 10 minutes, or until almost all liquid is absorbed.	5 minutes
Rice Brown, long grain	1 cup	2- to 3-quart casserole	Combine with 2 to 2½ cups liquid* (see package), 1 tablespoon oil, 1 teaspoon salt, if desired. Cover tightly. (Yield 3½ cups)	**High** 5–7 minutes, or to boiling. **Medium-Low** 45–55 minutes, or until liquid is absorbed.	5 minutes
White, long grain	1 cup	2- to 3-quart casserole	Combine with 1¾ to 2 cups liquid* (see package), 1 tablespoon oil, 1 teaspoon salt, if desired. Cover tightly. (Yields 3 cups.)	**High** 5–7 minutes or to boiling. **Medium** 15 minutes, or until liquid is absorbed	5 minutes
Brown or White, medium or short grain	1 cup	2- to 3-quart casserole	Combine with 1½ cups liquid*, 1 tablespoon oil, 1 teaspoon salt, if desired. Cover tightly.	**High** 5–7 minutes or to boiling. **Medium** 15 minutes, or until liquid is absorbed.	5 minutes
Basmati	1 cup	2- to 3-quart casserole	Combine with 1¾ cups liquid*, 1 tablespoon oil, ½ teaspoon salt, if desired. Cover tightly. (Yield 3½ cups.)	**High** 4–7 minutes, or to boiling. **Medium** 10 minutes, or until liquid is absorbed.	5 minutes

*Liquid may be water, stock, or fruit juice

BREAKFAST CEREALS

TYPE	AMOUNT**	CONTAINER	PREPARATION	COOKING TIME	STANDING TIME COVERED
Cornmeal	1 cup	2-quart casserole	Combine with 4 cups water and ½ teaspoon salt. Uncovered. Stir once.	**High** 4–6 minutes	2 minutes
Cream of Rice	⅔ cup	2-quart casserole	Combine with 2⅔ cups water and ½ teaspoon salt. Uncovered. Stir once.	**High** 3½–4½ minutes	2 minutes
Cream of Wheat	⅔ cup	3-quart casserole	Combine with 3¼ cups water and ½ teaspoon salt. Uncovered. Stir once.	**High** 7–8 minutes	2 minutes
Farina	⅔ cup	3-quart casserole	Combine with 3¼ cups water and ½ teaspoon salt. Uncovered. Stir once.	**High** 7–8 minutes	2 minutes
Grits (coarse cornmeal)	1 cup	3-quart casserole	Combine 3¼ cups water and ½ teaspoon salt. Cover tightly. Stir once.	**High** 8–10 minutes	2 minutes
Oat bran	1⅓ cups	2-quart casserole	Combine with 4 cups water and ¼ teaspoon salt. Uncovered. Stir well before serving.	**High** 8–9 minutes	1 minute
Oatmeal Old-fashioned	1⅓ cups	3-quart casserole	Combine with 2¾ cups water and ½ teaspoon salt. Uncovered. Stir once.	**High** 8–9 minutes	1 minute

(continued)

TYPE	AMOUNT**	CONTAINER	PREPARATION	COOKING TIME	STANDING TIME COVERED
Quick	1⅓ cups	2-quart casserole	Combine with 3 cups water and ½ teaspoon salt. Uncovered. Stir once.	**High** 5–6 minutes	None
Wheatena	1 cup	3-quart casserole	Combine with 3 cups water and ¼ teaspoon salt. Uncovered. Stir twice.	**High** 7–9 minutes	2 minutes

**For 4 servings.

INDEX

S

ABOUT THE AUTHOR

PAT BAIRD has been involved in the food and nutrition business her entire life. As a child, she worked in her father's retail—and then wholesale—food business. Her career was primed while she spent the next ten years working in the restaurant industry. She went on to get an M.A. in Nutrition and Dietetics; she is also a registered dietitian and a member of The American Dietetic Association. Since then she has been Administrative Dietitian at several leading New York hospitals and was Director of Food Services for a major public relations firm. Now a consultant for the food and health-care industries, she is also a spokesperson, writer, and adjunct university instructor. Pat Baird has contributed articles to *Ladies Home Journal,* the New York *Daily News*, and *Healthy Kids*. She resides in New York City and Los Angeles.